F

Danny,
Merry Christmas 1993
Dennis

Simon & Schuster's

GUIDE TO
Reptiles and Amphibians of the World

by
Massimo Capula

Photographs by Giuseppe Mazza

Edited by John L. Behler,
Curator of Herpetology,
New York Zoological Society

A FIRESIDE BOOK
PUBLISHED BY SIMON & SCHUSTER INC.
New York London Toronto Sydney Tokyo Singapore

ACKNOWLEDGMENTS

The author wishes to extend his warmest thanks to Professor Benedetto Lanza, Director of the "La Specola" Zoological Museum at the University of Florence.

This book is dedicated to Teresa and Giuseppe.

The photographer wishes to thank the following: Everglades Safari, Miami, USA; Everglades Wonder Gardens, Bonita Springs, USA; Fitzsimons Snake Park, Durban, South Africa; Mr Bruce Bednar, Miami, USA; Mr Joseph Fauci, Tampa, USA; Pet Farm, Miami, USA; Port Elizabeth Snake Park, Port Elizabeth, South Africa; Siam Zoo & Breeding Farm, Bangkok, Thailand; Thai Reptiles, Bangkok, Thailand; Mr Louis Porras, The Shed, Miami, USA; Australian Reptile Park, Gosford, Australia; Taronga Zoo, Sydney, Australia; Arizona-Sonora Desert Museum, Tucson, USA; Zoological Gardens of Sri Lanka, Colombo, Sri Lanka; National Zoological Gardens of South Africa, Pretoria, South Africa; Bredi's Reptile Park & Zoo, Rehmark, Australia. All the photographs are by Giuseppe Mazza except for the following: Mondadori Archives: p. 109; Steven C. Wilson-Entheos: pp. 106–107. Entries: M. Capula, 51, 52, 196; P. Carmichael/The Basic Foundation, Inc.: 47; J. Collins, the National Audubon Society Collection/PRI: 38; Panda Photo: 16, 23, 29, 202; Overseas (Jacana): 84.

Simon and Schuster/Fireside
Simon & Schuster Building
Rockefeller Center
1230 Avenue of the Americas
New York, New York 10020

Symbols by Grafica Service
Drawings by Vittorio Salarolo
Typeset by Rowland Phototypesetting Ltd, Bury St Edmunds, Suffolk, England
Printed and bound in Spain by Artes Gráficas Toledo, S. A.
D.L.TO:2135–1991
10 9 8 7 6 5 4 3 2 1
10 9 8 7 6 5 4 3   Pbk.

Library of Congress Cataloging in Publication Data
Capula, Massimo.
    [Tutto anfibi e rettili.   English]
    Simon & Schuster's guide to reptiles and amphibians of the world
  by Massimo Capula: photographs by Giusappe Mazza: edited by John
  L. Behler: [English translation by John Gilbert].
      p.   cm.
    Includes bibliographical references.
    ISBN 0-671-69136-8.—ISBN 0-671-69098-1 (A Fireside book: pbk.)
    1. Reptiles.   2. Amphibians.   I. Behler, John L.   II. Title.
III. Title: Guide to reptiles and amphibians of the world.
IV. Title: Simon and Schuster's guide to reptiles and amphibians of
the world.
QL641.C37131989
597.6—dc20   89-21671

CONTENTS

NOTE ON THE READING OF SYMBOLS

In this book each entry devoted to a species is provided with a series of symbols which indicate the habitats frequented, the life habits, and certain biological characteristics of the species concerned. Because the majority of species occupy more than one habitat, it is important to note that the symbolism adopted for these environments is purely indicative and approximate. So too are the symbols used to describe the life habits: in fact they show the prevalent period of activity of the species, although it may be that in certain regions of the range or at particular seasons the species will be active during periods other than those indicated.

NOTE ON THE READING OF ENTRIES

In the case of many amphibian and reptile species the systematic position is still under discussion. The names of the order, family, genus, and species which appear in this book are therefore based upon the most recent and up-to-date texts on the subject.

For the sake of convenience, the families within each order (or suborder) and the species within the families are listed in alphabetical sequence. For each species a minimum and maximum total length is given; the exception is in the case of species belonging to the order Chelonia (turtles and tortoises) for which it has seemed more opportune to provide instead the length of the carapace.

KEY TO SYMBOLS

Habitats frequented

lakes, swamps, ponds

rivers, streams

sea

caves, natural fissures

broadleaved woods,
temperate forests, scrub

tropical and
subtropical forests

prairies, savannas, steppes

desert, arid zones

mountains, rocky zones

Life habits

diurnal

crepuscular/nocturnal

Biological characteristics

partial neoteny

venomous species

Comparison between skull and forelimb of crossopterygian fishes (genus Eusthenopteron, *left) and of the labyrinthodont amphibians (genus* Eryops, *right).*

INTRODUCTION

During the Devonian period, more than 370 million years ago, an event of fundamental importance for the earth's animals took place: the colonization of dry land by certain animals, known as amphibians, who most likely were descended from a group of lobe-finned fishes belonging to the order Crossopterygii. The amphibians exhibited two distinct life phases, one larval, typically aquatic, the other meta-morphosed, aquatic or terrestrial. With four well-developed limbs, the Devonian amphibians were the first tetrapods, although they still displayed extraordinary affinities with their bonyfish ancestors, the Crossopterygians. Like the latter, they had channels of the lateral line on the outer surface of the skull bones, a vertebral column formed of two elements (the intercentrum and pleurocentrum), and teeth with numerous labyrinthine folds of enamel (a feature which led to the primitive amphibians being classified as the Labyrinthodontia).

From the ancestral stock of Paleozoic amphibians, two major branches are distinguishable at a fairly early stage, that of the Labyrinthodontia, spanning the Devonian to the Triassic periods, and the Lepospondyli, which lived during the Carboniferous and early Permian periods. The Labyrinthodont branch is certainly larger and more important, for it includes *Ichthyostega*, the earliest known

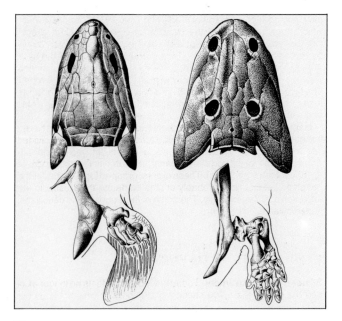

1) Skeleton of a salamander (genus Salamandra). *The body is elongated, there are numerous vertebrae and the tail is well developed. 2) Skeleton of a frog (genus* Rana). *The body is stocky, there are only seven vertebrae and the hind limbs are highly developed. There is no tail in the normal sense.*

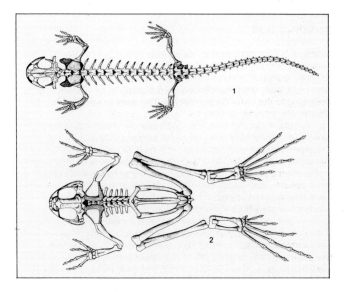

tetrapod, the Temnospondyli, probably ancestors of the Anura (frogs, etc.), and possibly of the other modern groups, and the anthracosaurs which became extinct at the close of the Permian period. Some anthracosaurs were quite reptile-like and may have been related to the ancestors of reptiles. The Lepospondyli is a strange group of diverse forms, some snake-like, some newt- or lizard-like, and some with grotesque flattened skulls drawn out behind into a pair of "horns." The lepospondyls may have died out without leaving descendants but it has been suggested that they included the ancestors of urodeles and caecilians.

Many structural differences and an enormous time-span separate the early tetrapods from present-day amphibians, which are divided into three orders: Caudata or Urodela (newts and salamanders), Anura or Salientia (frogs and toads), and the limbless Apoda or Gymnophiona (caecilians). These orders, grouped together under the heading Lissamphibia, probably originated during the Mesozoic era and evolved independently. The origin of the Caudata and caecilians, in particular, is still obscure.

BETWEEN WATER AND LAND:
ADAPTATIONS TO THE ENVIRONMENT

Structure and movement. Today the labyrinthodonts no longer exist and not one of the 4,100 species of amphibians which occupy our planet has teeth of labyrinthine structure. However, present-day amphibians are in some ways analogous to the primitive tetrapods which inhabited the land during the Paleozoic era. The Lissamphibia are ectothermic (having a variable body temperature determined by that of the environment), as the labyrinthodonts most probably were; also, they are virtually incapable of surviving in zones which completely lack fresh water, because it is here that they generally breed and undergo their larval development.

The amphibian skin, like that of vertebrates in general, consists of two main layers, the epidermis with its outer horny layer or stratum corneum, and the underlying dermis. The horny layer is an important aid against desiccation and is periodically shed and renewed. The epidermis possesses various glands which extend into the dermis; they can be divided into two categories, mucous and granular. The mucous glands are distributed all over the body and produce a slimy secretion that keeps the skin moist and facilitates respiration through it. The granular glands are located in particular parts of the body (e.g. the paratoid glands at the sides of the neck in many anurans and certain salamanders); their secretions are often poisonous. The dermis is well supplied with blood vessels, also essential in cutaneous respiration, and contains various pigment cells which determine the animal's color and in some cases are responsible for color change.

Each of the three orders of living amphibians exhibits a characteristic structural organization and skeletal system in relationship to its life habits and evolutionary path. The Apoda, which generally have burrowing habits, have a strong bony skull and a long cylindrical body divided into ringed segments. These worm-like amphibians possess a vertebral column composed of numerous vertebrae (up to 300). The tail is short or absent and there are no limbs, limb girdle vestiges or sternum.

The Caudata have a well developed tail and four limbs, except in the family Sirenidae where the hind legs are absent. As in Anura the skull is more open than in labyrinthodonts, so that regions of the brain-case (which remains partly unossified) are exposed. The sternum is a small cartilaginous plate. There are some 10–60 vertebrae in front of the sacrum, one sacral vertebra and 20–100 caudal vertebrae. The first (the "cervical") vertebra is modified for articulation with the skull. Aquatic Caudata swim by undulations of the body and tail, the latter being compressed from side to side. On land salamanders move by placing one front leg, say the left, forward followed by the right hind leg, and then vice versa.

The Anura lack a tail after metamorphosis and have hind legs that are longer and sturdier than the front ones. The vertebral column is differentiated into presacral, sacral and postsacral (caudal) regions. The presacral region of Anura is formed of 5–9 vertebrae, while the postsacral region consists of a single bone (the urostyle or coccyx) resulting from the fusion of those caudal vertebrae which are not lost during metamorphosis. The structure of the pectoral girdle is significant in classification. The hind legs, characterized among other things

Two phases of the movement of a salamander on dry land: a) the right front leg and the left hind leg are moved forward; b) then the left front leg and the right hind leg are moved forward.

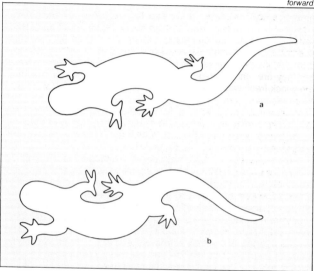

by a particularly long tarsus, are specialized for jumping and are provided with powerful extensor muscles. It is the contraction of these muscles which, in the case of land anurans, determines the length of the legs and thus the thrust of the feet against the ground which constitutes the jumping action. Aquatic anurans move by pushing the water backward with jerky kicks of the hind legs. These movements project the entire body of the animal rapidly forward.

As for body dimensions, the largest living amphibians are two caudates belonging to the family Cryptobranchidae: the Japanese giant salamander (*Andrias japonicus*), which can grow to a length of 4½ ft (1.4 m), and the Chinese giant salamander (*A. davidianus*), which exceptionally may reach a length of 6 ft (1.8 m). The smallest of living amphibians is the Cuban *Sminthillus limbatus*, also one of the Leptodactylidae, which grows to a maximum length of ½ in (12 mm).

Respiration and circulation. The respiratory tracts of amphibians begin with a pair of external nares (which communicate with the mouth cavity through the choanae or internal nares), the larynx, the trachea and (generally in larvae only) the gills. Although they normally breathe through their skin, metamorphosed amphibians are usually provided with lungs. These are matching sac-like organs which develop before the time of metamorphosis. Among the Anura and most of the Caudata, the size of the left and right lungs is roughly the same, but in the Apoda and Caudata belonging to the family

Amphiumidae, the left lung is fairly small and rudimentary. But certain caudates (all representatives of the family Plethodontidae and some species of Hynobiidae) lack lungs and breathe only through the skin and oral mucosa. In the larval stage, amphibians have four gill-slits and carry out gaseous exchanges through three pairs of external gills well supplied with blood vessels. The larvae of the Apoda and Caudata are furnished with large ramified gills at the sides of the head. In some forms, such as *Proteus*, the gills persist throughout life, the perennibranchiate condition. In the larvae of the Anura, however, the external gills disappear and internal gills develop, situated inside a peribranchial chamber which communicates with the outside by means of a small aperture (spiracle).

The structure of the breathing apparatus and the modifications it undergoes during metamorphosis are closely linked with the arrangement of circulatory system. In the larva before the lungs develop, the blood circulation is simple and the heart, characterized by a single atrium and a single ventricle, contains only venous blood. The blood sent from the sinus venosus into the atrium flows into the ventricle, which in its turn pumps it into the capillaries of the gills, where oxygenation occurs. After this the blood is ready to be circulated again. In metamorphosed individuals the heart is composed of three main chambers – two auricles and one ventricle. The venous blood from the body enters the right auricle via the sinus venosus, while the left auricle receives arterial blood from the lungs. The ventricle is undivided but there is relatively little mixing of oxygenated and deoxygenated blood within its cavity.

The nervous system and the sensory organs. As in vertebrates generally, the brain has three main divisions, the fore-, mid- and hindbrains. The cerebral hemispheres of the fore-brain are relatively large; their functions are still obscure, though they may play some part as correlating centers in connection with olfactory and visual impressions. Their olfactory lobes receive neurons from the sensory epithelium of the nose and from Jacobson's (vomeronasal) organ, an accessory organ of smell situated in the front part of each nasal cavity. The mid-brain is well developed, receiving fibers from the optic and auditory systems and "sending" fibers to the lower centers such as the medulla. It is important in movement and behavior. The cerebellum is small, perhaps because most amphibians have no great need for speed or balance. There are 10 (or 11, depending on terminology) pairs of cranial nerves, the more posterior of which arise from the elongated medulla. (The 12th [hypoglossal] nerve of higher vertebrates which supplies the tongue muscles is here derived from the first one or two spinal nerves.)

The eye in aquatic larval and adult amphibians which do not fully metamorphose has general resemblances to that of fishes. In other amphibians eyelids and eye glands which keep the cornea moist are developed at or before metamorphosis. In the Apoda and in certain cave-dwelling Caudata belonging to the families Plethodontidae and

Proteidae the eyes are much reduced and covered by a thin layer of skin. The Anura as a rule have large protruding eyes characterized by a multiform pupil; according to the species it may be round, triangular, heart-shaped or in the form of a vertical or horizontal slit. The Apoda are provided with a tiny retractable "tentacle" between the eye and the nostril on each side. This almost certainly helps to register olfactory sensations. The larvae of many Caudata and of those Anura which live permanently in water are able to pick up vibrations in this element like fishes and primitive amphibians, by means of organs of the lateral line. Such organs are located on the head and at the sides of the body and are known as neuromasts. Many Anura have a tympanic membrane (ear drum) and middle ear, across which sound vibrations are transmitted by an ossicle, the columella, to the inner ear. Tympanic membrane and middle ear are absent in Caudata and Apoda. Most present-day amphibians have an additional ossicle called the operculum applied to the inner ear which is connected by a muscle with the scapula in anurans and most caudates. It is often said that this provides a means of transmitting ground vibrations through the fore-legs, but in frogs, at least, the mechanism may be concerned with balance.

LIFE AND HABITS

Food. The vitellus or yolk in the egg of amphibians is rich in nutritive substances and represents the first source of food available to the animals. After hatching the larvae have to search for food actively in the surrounding water. Salamander larvae are essentially carnivorous and have jaws with teeth capable of grasping tiny insects, small crustaceans, and other invertebrates which are sucked into the mouth together with the water. The larvae of Anura are, by contrast, typically vegetarian. In the majority of families belonging to this order the tadpoles have special mouth structures designed to rake algae and plant detritus from the surface of submerged objects. The strangest feature of these structures is undoubtedly the beak, situated in the center of the mouth and formed of a horny upper portion and a similar lower part. This beak is normally surrounded by other rasp-like structures, known as false labial teeth, derived from the cornification of the buccal epithelium and arranged in rows above and below the beak. However, the tadpoles of the Pipidae, Rhinophrynidae and Microhylidae have no beak or "teeth," but are provided with a filter on the inner side of the gill arches which retain particulate matter (microorganisms in suspension) sucked into the mouth along with water. The food particles, raked or filtered, are normally conveyed to the intestine which, in all anuran tadpoles, is fairly long and spiral-shaped.

Adult amphibians are all carnivores and feed mainly on annelid worms, crustaceans, spiders and insects. The bigger species, however, often prey as well on small reptiles, other amphibians or tiny mammals. They usually catch prey with their large, mobile tongue. In

Copulation in frogs. 1) Lumbar copulation (genus Discoglossus*); 2) Axillary copulation (genus* Bufo*)*

many Anura the forward portion of the tongue is fixed to the floor of the mouth, while the rear portion is free and, when extended, can be suddenly flipped over. Some salamanders, on the other hand, have a sticky, mushroom-shaped tongue (beletoid tongue) which is projected at the prey with a movement like that of a chameleon. Amphibians without a tongue (anurans of the family Pipidae) and those furnished with a simple fleshy fold on the floor of the mouth (certain species of Caudata) grasp the victim only with their small teeth.

In the majority of Apoda and Caudata, there are teeth in both jaws whereas in the Anura they are found only in the upper jaw. The prey is swallowed with the aid of mucous secretions from glands located in the buccal epithelium, and conveyed from the esophagus to the stomach, where the digestive processes occur. Absorption of food substances takes place in the intestine, while elimination of products that cannot be assimilated is effected by the cloaca, which forms the terminal part of the rectum and which also includes the terminal parts of the genital and urinary tracts. In the Apoda, the Caudata and tadpoles of the Anura, the cloacal aperture is situated ventrally, at the base of the tail, whereas in the metamorphosed Anura it is positioned terminally at the rear.

The type and amount of food consumed daily is strictly related to the individual species' life phase and habits. As a rule the larvae have fairly high growth rhythms and feed almost continuously. The adults, however, feed more sparingly and show restraint even when prey is hard to come by; and in regions where there is a marked seasonal

16

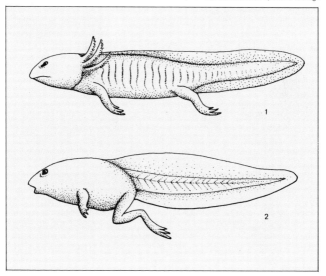

difference in climate they are able to remain in a latent condition (diapause), feeding exclusively on stocks of energy accumulated at times of maximum activity.

Reproduction. Depending on the climate and the altitude of the region inhabited, amphibians will either reproduce at only one determined time of year or will have several seasonal spawning periods. As a rule the two sexes come together in or near the water, but certain species couple on land. Fertilization is internal in most Caudata, the Hynobiidae and Cryptobranchidae being the exceptions. However, mating, apart from rare cases, does not involve amplexus or the direct transference of sperm from male to female by means of a copulatory organ.

Males of the Caudata may take on a distinctive livery (dorsal crests, caudal and digital membranes, etc.) and exceptionally bright colors during the courtship period, and they perform nuptial dances of varying complexity to stimulate the females. At the climax of these ceremonies they emit masses of sperm wrapped in gelatinous capsules (spermatophores) which are retrieved by the females' cloacal lips. In the Apoda, fertilization is likewise internal but the males of these amphibians do not produce spermatophores, being equipped with a protrusible cloaca which, functioning as a copulatory organ, allows sperm to be transferred directly into the female's cloaca.

Among virtually all the Anura, fertilization is external. The males do not perform a nuptial dance but call and conquer the females by singing. They possess a large pharynx and either one or two vocal sacs in the throat or at the sides of the head, which, when they sing, are inflated with air and function as sound-boxes. After the preliminary tentative courtship calls, the males leap onto the backs of the females and clasp them with their forelegs in an embrace (amplexus), either beneath the armpits (axillary amplexus) or around the loins (lumbar amplexus); meanwhile they spray sperm over the eggs emitted by the females. Exceptions to this rule among the Anura, where sperm is introduced directly into the female's cloaca, are found in males belonging to species of the African genus *Nectophrynoides*, which simply juxtapose their cloaca with that of their partner, and males of the North American *Ascaphus truei*, which have an outward-turned cloaca which functions as a copulatory organ.

An amphibian's egg contains a fairly large yolk (mesolecithal egg) which is mainly concentrated ventrally. Species with oviparous reproduction lay free eggs in clusters or gelatinous chains, either in the water, on wet ground, beneath leaves or inside foam nests. In some cases the eggs are retained and carried about by one of the parents (for example by the male in *Alytes obstetricans* of the Discoglossidae) until they hatch; alternatively they may develop wholly or partially in special areas of the mother's body (e.g. the cells scattered through the dorsal region of the females of certain South American Anura belonging to the genus *Pipa*) or of the father's body (e.g. the vocal sacs of the males of the South American anuran *Rhinoderma darwinii*).

The larvae hatch from the eggs laid in the water after a period that varies, according to species, from 24 hours to several weeks. The larvae of the Caudata, whose forelegs develop prior to the hind legs, and of the Apoda, are quite similar to metamorphosed individuals. The larvae of the Anura have an oval body and a fairly long tail, and their hind legs develop before the front pair. The larval phase is of variable duration, depending on climatic factors and the amount of food available, from a few days to more than a year. The larvae of certain amphibians will nevertheless remain unaltered throughout life (total neoteny) or for a longer than normal period (partial neoteny). Among the Caudata some individuals will reach sexual maturity although permanently retaining a number of larval characteristics (obligatory, almost obligatory or facultative paedogenesis).

Species with ovoviviparous or viviparous reproduction give birth to larvae which are either close to metamorphosis or which are already metamorphosed and in all respects like the adults. In both cases the fertilized eggs are retained inside the mother's body, but whereas in ovoviviparity the embryo develops by feeding exclusively on the yolk content, in viviparity the embryo obtains part of its food from certain of the mother's tissues (the walls of Müller's ducts) which function like the placenta of higher vertebrates.

Habitats. Amphibians are distributed over all continents except Antarctica. They frequent all the principal land and water habitats of the planet and are found, mainly at night or in rainy weather, in

Phases in the development of a frog (Rana temporaria) *from top to bottom and left to right: egg with developing embryos; newly hatched tadpoles; tadpoles at beginning of larval development (the external gills are still present); tadpole at advanced stage of larval development (the rudiments of the hind legs are already evident); recently metamorphosed individual (the residue of a tail is still visible); adult individual.*

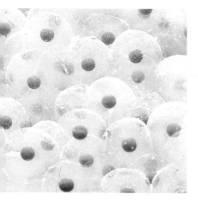

ponds, streams, woods and even caves. However, amphibians cannot tolerate the high salt content of sea water and are therefore the only vertebrates not to have colonized marine habitats. Nevertheless certain Anura (e.g. *Bufo arenarum* and *B. viridis*) breed in brackish swamps and, at least after metamorphosis, manage to live even in waters with a concentration of sodium chloride equivalent to 20 grams per liter.

Amphibians mainly populate temperate and tropical regions but it is principally in the latter zones that one finds the greatest number of species and the widest range of adaptations to various kinds of life (arboreal, terrestrial and aquatic). Leaping from branch to branch is performed by many treefrogs. A few species like *Hyla miliaria*, *Agalychnis moreletii*, and various *Rhacophorus*, are capable of "parachuting" or gliding.

In the tropical regions of South America live the singular representatives of the family Typhlonectidae, the only known apodans that are exclusively aquatic. Some amphibians are admirably adapted for life even in areas with exceptionally unfavorable climatic conditions and surroundings. The Australian anurans *Cyclorana platycephala* and *Notaden nichollsi*, for example, are typical desert-dwelling amphibians, while the Asiatic caudate *Hynobius keyserlingii* and the North American anuran *Rana sylvatica* inhabit regions that for several months a year are subject to very low temperatures. Moreover, certain amphibians live in mountainous zones, some species being found at extremely high altitudes: in Europe, for instance, the alpine salamander (*Salamandra atra*) normally lives at heights of between 2,000 and 3,000 m (6,500 and 10,000 ft), while in South America the aquatic anurans of the genus *Telmatobius* inhabit the freezing lakes of the Andes range at altitudes of between 3,000 and 4,000 m (10,000 and 13,500 ft).

In regions with a temperate or temperate-arctic climate, amphibians experience a dramatic slowing down of metabolic processes with the onset of winter. As a result they enter a phase of latency, for varying lengths of time, often described as hibernation, which enables these ectothermic animals to spend the winter unharmed inside burrows dug in the ground or beneath the mud at the bottom of ponds. Amphibians which inhabit tropical zones characterized by particularly hot, dry seasons are likewise subject to a period of latency, but in this case the slowed metabolism serves to protect these animals from very high temperatures and from drought.

INTRODUCTION TO CLASSIFICATION

Classification and distribution of amphibians. The majority of herpetologists divide the classes of amphibians into three subclasses: the Labyrinthodontia, the Lepospondyli and the Lissamphibia. The first two consist exclusively of species that have been extinct for at least two hundred million years and are therefore known only from

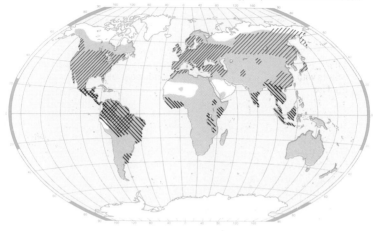

Distribution of amphibians on earth: the distribution area of frogs is shown in yellow, that of salamanders in red and that of gymnophionans caecilians in black.

palaeontological documentation, while the third includes all living species. The subclass Lissamphibia is fairly composite and probably does not represent a monophyletic grouping. In fact, it comprises four orders that differ considerably from one another from osteological and morphological viewpoints: the Proanura (whose representatives are known only in the fossil state), the Apoda, the Caudata, and the Anura.

The classification of living amphibians adopted in this book follows that proposed in the *Encyclopedia of Reptiles and Amphibians* edited by T. Halliday and K. Adler (1986), William E. Duellman and Linda Trueb, 1986. This classification is modified in respect of certain families of Caudata and Anura, based on the work of C. J. Goin, O. B. Goin and G. R. Zug (1978), and W. E. Duellman and L. Trueb (1986).

PROTECTION

Principal causes of amphibian rarity and problems of protection.
Today, principally as a result of pollution and thoughtless destruction of wetlands, survival for a growing number of amphibian species depends almost entirely on the extension and preservation of limited protected areas set up by individual countries to save the last remaining outposts of the natural environment. The amphibians, in fact, are associated with wet regions by strict physiological necessity and are thus more affected than other vertebrates by serious human encroachment on their habitats. However, the poisoning and devastation of wetlands are not the only threats to the survival of these

21

animals: there is also direct human persecution for commercial reasons (collection, gastronomic interest, breeding, etc.) or simply from fear. Many people, quite unjustifiably, have a feeling of dislike for amphibians and this does not help to popularize initiatives taken to safeguard their future. The economic and moral sacrifices that are needed to protect these vertebrates, at least within areas set aside for that purpose, would not be onerous and would be compensated for much greater ecological benefits. All the Anura, for example, are formidable enemies of "harmful" insects and in their turn constitute an essential source of food for a large number of reptiles, birds, and mammals. According to information contained in the *Red Data Book* of animal species threatened with extinction, there are today some 45 species of amphibians (21 Caudata and 24 Anura) which are likely to vanish from the face of the earth if the factors of disturbance responsible for their dramatic decline persist. In order to protect these and other endangered populations, international conventions and particular countries have enacted laws prohibiting or at least controlling the capture and trading of rare species. But only in a few cases are these regulations strictly and immediately enforced so that their effectiveness is obviously compromised. Moreover, laws and international conventions, although they represent a first significant step in the protection of these animals, cannot and should not be the only

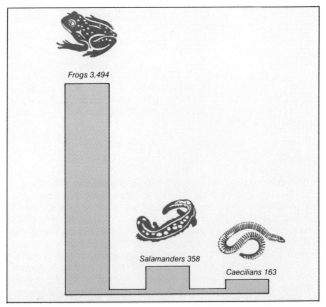

Frogs 3,494

Salamanders 358

Caecilians 163

instruments for ensuring the survival of amphibians on our planet. Indeed, the future of these animals depends above all on our own desire and determination to conserve, effectively and lastingly, the environment in which we live; and this will happen only when there is a radical change in our traditional attitude of stubborn repulsion toward these little known and very attractive creatures.

Table 1

Order APODA (Gymnophiona)
    Fam. Caeciliidae
        Central and South America, sub-Saharan Africa,
        Seychelles, southern India
    Fam. Ichthyophiidae
        Southeast Asia
    Fam. Uraeothyphlidae
        Southern India
    Fam. Rhinatrematidae
        South America
    Fam. Scolecomorphidae
        Cameroon, Tanzania
    Fam. Typhlonectidae
        South America

Order CAUDATA (Urodela)
    Fam. Cryptobranchidae
        Eastern United States and eastern China, Japan
    Fam. Hynobiidae
        European Russia, Palearctic Asia, Southeast Asia
    Fam. Salamandridae
        North America, Europe, northwest Africa, Asia
    Fam. Amphiumidae
        Southeastern United States
    Fam. Proteidae
        Eastern and central North America, northeastern Italy,
        western Yugoslavia
    Fam. Ambystomatidae
        North America
    Fam. Dicamptodontidae
        Pacific coast, North America
    Fam. Sirenidae
        Eastern United States and northeastern Mexico

Order ANURA (Salientia)
    Fam. Leiopelmatidae
        New Zealand and western North America
    Fam. Discoglossidae
        Europe, northwest Africa, Asia Minor, eastern Asia,
        Philippines, Borneo
    Fam. Pipidae
        South America, Africa
    Fam. Rhinophrynidae
        Central America, Mexico, south Texas
    Fam. Pelobatidae
        North America, Europe, northwest Africa, Asia Minor,
        Southeast Asia

Fam. Pelodytidae
Western Europe and southwestern Asia
Fam. Bufonidae
North, Central and South America, Europe, Africa, Asia
Fam. Brachycephalidae
Southeastern Brazil
Fam. Rhinodermatidae
Southern Chile, southern Argentina
Fam. Heleophrynidae
Southern Africa
Fam. Myobatrachidae
Australia, Tasmania, New Guinea
Fam. Leptodactylidae
Extreme southern regions of North America, Central and South America
Fam. Dendrobatidae
Central and South America
Fam. Hylidae
North, Central, and South America, Europe, North Africa, Asia, New Guinea, Australia
Fam. Centrolenidae
Central and South America
Fam. Pseudidae
South America
Fam. Ranidae
North, Central and South America, Europe, Africa, Asia, Indonesia, New Guinea, northeastern Australia
Fam. Sooglossidae
Seychelles
Fam. Hyperoliidae
Central and southern Africa, Madagascar, Seychelles
Fam. Rhacophoridae
Central and southern Africa, southern Asia, Indonesia, Philippines, Japan
Fam. Microhylidae
North, Central, and South America, central and southern Africa, Southeast Asia, New Guinea, northeastern Australia

1 DERMOPHIS MEXICANUS
Mexican caecilian

Classification   Order Gymnophiona, Family Caeciliidae.
Distribution   Central America, from southern Mexico to Panama.
Identification   The front of the head is pointed and triangular in shape. The eyes are covered by skin and a small tentacle which enhances the sense of smell is found in a depression below and in front of the eye. The limbs are absent and the relatively long, stocky body bears numerous and conspicuous annular rings. The tail is virtually nonexistent, the body ending in a blunt point. The back is grayish or olive-brown and the belly usually yellowish. There is a prominent yellow spot on the cloacal region. Total length: 16–24 in (40–60 cm).
Habitat   Moist soils with plenty of ground litter.
Biology   This worm-like amphibian is for the most part a burrower and surfaces only at night and on rainy days. It digs rapidly, hunting insects, termites, and earthworms in underground tunnels. Strong jaws and numerous small hooked teeth enable it to grasp and swallow prey. The species is viviparous, each female giving birth on the ground to 3–4 young, similar in all respects to the adults but only two inches long.

---

2 ICHTHYOPHIS GLUTINOSUS
Ceylonese caecilian

Classification   Order Gymnophiona, Family Ichthyophiidae.
Distribution   Sri Lanka.
Identification   The head is oval and relatively small. The eyes are minute, covered by skin, but visible. A tiny finger-like, chemical-detecting tentacle is situated between the eye and nostril, near the edge of the upper lip. There are no limbs and the body displays 350–390 annular rings, very close to one another. The conical tail is very short. The color of the back is uniformly dark brown with a few violet tints, and the belly is somewhat paler. A yellow stripe extends along the flanks from head to tail. Total length: 12–16 in (30–40 cm).
Habitat   Muddy and swampy ground close to water.
Biology   The species lives in tunnels, not too far from the surface, dug in the mud. Food consists mainly of earthworms and various arthropods. After mating, the female digs a burrow close to water and lays as many as 54 eggs there. She coils herself around the eggs until they hatch. The newborn larvae immediately head for nearby ponds or streams and remain there until they complete metamorphosis.

3 AMBYSTOMA MACULATUM
Spotted salamander

Classification Order Caudata, Family Ambystomatidae.
Distribution Eastern North America, from Ontario and Nova Scotia to Georgia and Texas.
Identification This salamander is black, blue-black or brownish, with two conspicuous irregular rows of round, yellow or orange spots which extend from head to tail. The underside is uniformly gray. The body is robust, with 12 distinct costal grooves on the sides. Total length: 6–9¾ in (15–25 cm). (9¾ in = record size.)
Habitat Deciduous woods close to small ponds and pools.
Biology The species spends most of its life underground. Adults move to the mouth of their tunnels at night or on particularly rainy days, to ambush earthworms and other passing small invertebrates. In winter or at the beginning of spring rains, sexually mature individuals migrate to ponds to breed. The females lay one or more masses containing about 50–100 eggs. The larvae hatch in 1–2 months.

4 AMBYSTOMA TIGRINUM
Tiger salamander

Classification Order Caudata, Family Ambystomatidae.
Distribution North America, from Canada to Mexico.
Identification Largest of the land-dwelling salamanders, it is stoutly built and has a broad head with small eyes. The back is dark brown or blackish, with numerous light patches, varying in shape and arrangement, but sometimes fused with one another to form transverse stripes. The sides of the body have 11–14 distinct costal grooves. The relatively long tail is compressed laterally. Total length: 6–14 in (15–35 cm).
Habitat Arid plains and pine barrens to wet meadows and mountain forests.
Biology Adults spend most of the day under plant detritus or in abandoned crayfish or mammal burrows. During the night, especially after heavy rainstorms, they leave their shelters and surface to look for small tasty prey such as earthworms and snails. Breeding occurs at the end of winter or in early spring in temporary pools or fishless waters. The females lay jelly-like masses of 50–100 eggs on submerged debris. The larvae hatch within about one month and undergo metamorphosis in the summer.

5 DICAMPTODON ENSATUS
Pacific giant salamander

Classification Order Caudata, Family Ambystomatidae.
Distribution Southeastern British Columbia, coastal northwestern United States, northern Idaho.
Identification This salamander has a fairly robust head and large protruding eyes. The back is generally brown, with abundant blackish marbling; the underside is light brown or yellowish. The tail is always highly compressed laterally. Total length: 8–12 in (20–30 cm).
Habitat Cool humid forests near small rivers and streams.
Biology Terrestrial adults are found under leaf litter, logs, and rocks. They are extremely voracious and although they normally hunt small prey such as earthworms and insects, will readily attack and devour other salamanders and even small snakes. In spring, sexually mature individuals move to stream headwaters where the males court the females. Eggs are laid singly and are attached to submerged logs or rocks. The larvae may metamorphose in their second year when they are about 4–6 in (10–15 cm) long. Some larvae never transform to the land stage. They become aquatic but retain their larval bushy gills.

6 AMPHIUMA MEANS
Two-toed amphiuma

Classification Order Caudata, Family Amphiumidae.
Distribution Southeastern United States, coastal plain from Virginia to Louisiana.
Identification An eel-like salamander with four tiny legs each with two toes. The head is flattened with a blunt snout and small, lidless eyes. The tail is cylindrical at the base, laterally compressed near the tip. The back is dark gray or gray-brown, while the underparts are lighter. Total length: 18–46 in (45–116 cm).
Habitat Swamps, marshes, and ditches with stagnant or slow-moving water.
Biology The "Congo eel" is ill-tempered and exclusively aquatic, spending the day hidden beneath submerged vegetation. At night it leaves its shelter and searches for crayfish, frogs, fish, and small snakes. The female lays a long bead-like chain of about 200 eggs in a cavity that she has dug in the mud. She remains coiled around the eggs until the larvae hatch approximately five months later.

7 ANDRIAS JAPONICUS
Japanese giant salamander

Classification Order Caudata, Family Cryptobranchidae.
Distribution Kyushu Island and western Honshu Island, Japan.
Identification This aquatic species is among the largest of the salamanders. The head is broad and very flat. The eyes are small, without lids. There are 15 costal grooves on the flattened body, and there is a large flap of skin along the sides. The tail is short and laterally compressed. The limbs are short and stocky. The color is uniformly brown or gray, with several irregularly arranged dark spots. During the breeding season the male's cloacal region is swollen. Total length: 39–57 in (100–144 cm).
Habitat Cool, clear rivers and streams in hill and mountain regions.
Biology This species is exclusively aquatic. During the day it remains hidden in a dark shelter on the stream bottom. At night it comes out to stalk fish, other amphibians and crustaceans. In the breeding season, August–September, the female lays long strings of eggs and the male, after fertilizing them, stays to guard them until they hatch in 2 to 3 months. The larval phase lasts three years.

8 ANEIDES AENEUS
Green salamander

Classification Order Caudata, Family Plethodontidae.
Distribution Eastern United States, from southwestern Pennsylvania to central Alabama.
Identification The head is large and flat, with big protruding eyes. The relatively flat body has 14–15 costal grooves. Toe tips are expanded and squarish. The tail is cylindrical. The upper parts are black with numerous green or yellow-green blotches. Total length: 3¼–5½ in (8–14 cm).
Habitat Sandstone rock outcrops with plenty of damp crevices and under bark of rotting trees.
Biology The green salamander is exclusively terrestrial and spends the day in a favorite retreat. By night it explores for small arthropod prey on vertical rock walls and tree trunks. Mating occurs from May to August. The female lays a cluster of 10–20 eggs in a rock crevice and stays to protect them until they hatch. There is no aquatic larval phase, and the young, less than 1 in (2 cm), are miniatures of the adults.

9 BATRACHOSEPS ATTENUATUS
Californian slender salamander

Classification   Order Caudata, Family Plethodontidae.
Distribution   Far western United States, southwestern Oregon, California.
Identification   The head is tiny, with large protruding eyes. The body and the tail are extremely long and cylindrical. There are 18–22 costal grooves. The limbs are short and weak; each limb has four small toes. The color is very variable, but normally the upper parts are blackish, with a wide yellowish brown or reddish stripe running from head to tail tip. The underside is brown or black, finely speckled with white. Total length: 3–5½ in (8–14 cm).
Habitat   Moist coastal mountains, redwood forests, interior foothills, and savannas.
Biology   This salamander is commonly encountered during rainy periods. It lives in leaf litter and the channels of rotted-out tree roots. On cool, rainy nights it leaves its shelters and hunts for earthworms and insects. Mating takes place in winter, when each female lays 4–21 eggs in small depressions underneath stones and logs. The entire larval development occurs inside the eggs, and the young hatch in spring.

10 BOLITOGLOSSA MEXICANA
Mexican lungless salamander

Classification   Order Caudata, Family Plethodontidae.
Distribution   Veracruz, Mexico to Honduras.
Identification   This salamander has a small, bluntly pointed head. The body is flat and there are 13 prominent costal grooves. The limbs are short and stocky. The toes of the front and back feet are linked by large webs. The color is extremely variable, but as a rule the upper parts are black with two rows of yellow spots, which are sometimes fused to form two continuous bands running from head to tail. The sides are uniformly dark; the belly is black or brownish with a few small white spots. Total length: 5½–7½ in (14–19 cm).
Habitat   Densely vegetated mountain slopes.
Biology   During the day it remains hidden under stones or the bark of fallen trees; at night it ventures out to hunt earthworms and small arthropods. It is an excellent climber and uses this ability especially in the dry parts of the year, when it seeks out various shrubby bromeliads which hold water. The eggs are laid in a hole on the ground or in rotting tree stumps, and the mother stays to look after them until the young hatch.

11 DESMOGNATHUS QUADRAMACULATUS
Black-bellied salamander

Classification   Order Caudata, Family Plethodontidae.
Distribution   Eastern United States, from West Virginia to Georgia.
Identification   The head is flat, with large protruding eyes. The body, supported by short, sturdy legs, has 14 distinct costal grooves on the sides. The tail is cylindrical at the base and highly compressed laterally towards the tip. The upper parts are black with numerous greenish marks of various shapes and patterns. There are two rows of white spots along the flanks. The underparts are uniformly black or dark brown. Total length: 3½–8¼ in (9–21 cm).
Habitat   Swift moving mountain streams with stony or pebbly beds.
Biology   This largely aquatic salamander is a good swimmer and rarely travels far from the stream. Though nocturnal, it is occasionally seen basking on wet rocks during the day. At night it leaves its retreat and hunts insects, molluscs, and small salamanders. The breeding season begins in late spring and lasts until July. The female lays 15–40 eggs, attaching them singly to the lower surface of submerged rocks or stones. The eggs hatch in late summer and the larvae metamorphose when they are 2½–3½ in (6–9 cm) long.

12 EURYCEA BISLINEATA
Two-lined salamander

Classification   Order Caudata, Family Plethodontidae.
Distribution   Eastern North America.
Identification   The body is slender and flat, with 13–16 costal grooves on either side. The tail is longer than the body, keeled, and laterally compressed. The head is tiny, with protruding eyes. There is a broad golden band along the back, from neck to tail, flanked on each side by a black line. In some populations, however, there are marked color variations: the dorsal band may be chestnut, green or reddish, and the two lateral lines may dissolve around the tail area into a series of small black spots. Total length: 2½–4¾ in (6–12 cm).
Habitat   Spring seepages, rocky brooks, river swamps, and rivulets in mountain forests.
Biology   The species is mainly aquatic and spends the day hidden under submerged rocks. It is a good swimmer and flees rapidly if disturbed, concealing itself beneath stones and other objects on the stream bed. It feeds on tiny insects and crustaceans. In the breeding season each female lays 20–100 eggs, attaching them to submerged stones or water plants. The larval phase lasts 1–3 years.

13 EURYCEA LONGICAUDA
Long-tailed salamander

Classification   Order Caudata, Family Plethodontidae.
Distribution   Eastern United States from southern New York to Florida panhandle.
Identification   The slender body has 13–14 costal grooves on each side. The tail is laterally compressed and much longer than the body. The coloration of the upper parts is extremely variable: in populations inhabiting northern regions of the range, the back and the tail are yellowish or red-orange, with numerous small black spots; southern populations, however, have a wide golden band with a dark vertebral stripe which is flanked by two wide black bands. Total length: 4–7⅞ in (10–20 cm).
Habitat   Stream margins, spring runs, cave openings, and wooded floodplains.
Biology   This species is less dependent on water than the two-lined salamander and is found during the day under fallen trunks and stones. On rainy nights it emerges to hunt small invertebrates. Breeding occurs from October to March, when the female lays her eggs in ground crevices with ready access to the beds of streams and springs. The eggs hatch in 6–8 weeks and the larval phase lasts 3½–7 months.

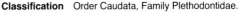

14 GYRINOPHILUS PORPHYRITICUS
Spring salamander

Classification   Order Caudata, Family Plethodontidae.
Distribution   Eastern North America, from Quebec to Georgia and Mississippi.
Identification   The head is fairly long, with slightly protruding eyes. A light line runs from eye to nostril. The sturdy body has 17–19 costal grooves on either side. The tail is keeled. The upper parts are salmon-red or pinkish-brown with a variable pattern of dark dots or reticulations. The underparts are often stippled with silver-white. Total length: 4½–8⅝ in (11–22 cm).
Habitat   Mountain streams and springs with cool, clear water.
Biology   This salamander is an excellent swimmer. It spends the day among submerged vegetation or beneath stones on the stream bed. During heavy showers at night it sometimes leaves the water to hunt small prey such as salamanders on the bank. Arthropods are their principal diet and are caught in the water. The breeding season occurs in summer, when each female lays 11–100 eggs, attaching them separately to the lower surface of submerged stones. The larval stage lasts two to three years.

15　HEMIDACTYLIUM SCUTATUM
Four-toed salamander

Classification　Order Caudata, Family Plethodontidae.
Distribution　Eastern North America, east of the Mississippi River, from Wisconsin to Nova Scotia and south to the Gulf.
Identification　The head is short and flat, with small protruding eyes. The legs are short and delicate with four toes on each foot. There are 13–14 costal grooves on either side of the body. The tail is laterally compressed, with a marked constriction at the base. For this reason the tail can easily be broken off if the animal is threatened or injured by a predator, as in many lizards. The color of the back is reddish-brown while the sides are grayish. Total length: 2–4 in (5–10 cm).
Habitat　Boggy wetlands, floodplains, and moist mossy woodlands.
Biology　This salamander is found in leaf litter and under stones or in dense sphagnum moss surrounding the water where it breeds. In the breeding season the female attaches her eggs to plants and tends them until they hatch. The aquatic larval stage lasts 1–2 months.

16　HYDROMANTES ITALICUS
Italian cave salamander

Classification　Order Caudata, Family Plethodontidae.
Distribution　Southeastern France, northern and central Italy.
Identification　The head is flat, with large protruding eyes. There is a thin nasal-labial groove under each nostril. The tail is cylindrical. The feet are partly webbed with short blunt toes. The dorsal coloration is very variable: dark brown, reddish or ocher, with pinkish or light brown patches or spots. The underparts are usually dark, often with whitish marbling. The male has an oval gland on the chin. Total length: 3¼–5¼ in (8–13 cm).
Habitat　Natural and man-made cavities, crevices, wet and vertical rock faces with many fissures.
Biology　The species is found on calcareous, cracked rocks and the wet walls of caves. It is nocturnally active, especially after heavy rain. It uses its long, flexible tongue for catching small insects and spiders. Mating, preceded by a complex courtship ritual, occurs in late winter. The female lays 5–10 eggs in rock clefts and stays to tend them until they hatch. There is no aquatic larval phase and the young hatch after 12 months.

17 PLETHODON CINEREUS
Red-backed salamander

Classification   Order Caudata, Family Plethodontidae.
Distribution   Eastern North America, from Ontario and Newfoundland in the north, to Indiana and North Carolina in the south.
Identification   The head is tiny, with large protruding eyes. The body is cylindrical and fairly long, with 19 costal grooves on either side. The legs are feeble. The tail is long and cylindrical. There are two color phases: the "red-backed" has a broad, red stripe from head onto tail. The stripe may also be yellow-orange, pink, or gray. "Head-backed" specimens are light gray to black. Total length: 2½–5 in (6–12 cm).
Habitat   Mixed broadleaf woods, coniferous forests, suburban gardens.
Biology   This terrestrial species is found amid woodland litter. By day or in dry periods it remains inactive, concealed under stones or in underground burrows. It can withstand cold and on very wet nights leaves its shelters to search for tiny invertebrates. In June or July the female attaches a small cluster of gelatinous eggs to the underside of a stone and coils about them until they hatch in two months. There is no aquatic larval phase.

---

18 PLETHODON GLUTINOSUS
Slimy salamander

Classification   Order Caudata, Family Plethodontidae.
Distribution   Eastern United States, from New York southward to Florida, westward to Oklahoma and Texas.
Identification   The head is broad and flat, with protruding eyes. The body is elongated, with 16 costal grooves. The tail is longer than the body and cylindrical. The upper parts are glossy black with a sprinkling of small silvery white marks. There are numerous large white or gray spots on the flanks. Total length: 4½–8 in (11–20 cm).
Habitat   Lowland forests, shaded ravines, damp shale banks, caves.
Biology   This terrestrial species has similar habits to *Plethodon cinereus*. It is active mainly at night, especially after heavy rains. When disturbed or attacked, its skin emits a sticky glandular secretion like glue, which probably makes the animal distasteful to predators. During the breeding season the female lays 3–36 eggs in small underground burrows and stays to look after them until they hatch. There is no aquatic larval stage and the hatchlings, ¾–1¼ in (2–3 cm) are in every way like the adults.

19 PSEUDOTRITON RUBER
Red salamander

Classification Order Caudata, Family Plethodontidae.
Distribution Eastern United States, from New York westward to Indiana, southward to Alabama and Mississippi.
Identification The species has a small head with tiny yellow eyes. The body, on short, stocky legs, is quite stout, while the tail is short and almost cylindrical. In the young the upper parts are coral- or orange-red, with scattered small black spots, irregularly arranged. In the adults the back is reddish-brown or chestnut with purple tints. Total length: 4–7 in (10–18 cm). Costal grooves = 16–17.
Habitat Springs, cold, clear brooks, swamps, and surrounding woodlands.
Biology This splendid salamander is usually seen in or near aquatic situations, but it is sometimes encountered, particularly at night or on very rainy days, some distance from water. In warm, dry periods it remains inactive and hides under rocks or plant detritus. It eats insects and earthworms. Breeding takes place in autumn, the female laying 50–100 eggs in small cavities beneath submerged stones. The larval phase lasts about two years and the young metamorphose when they are 2¾–4 in (7–10) cm long.

20 NECTURUS MACULOSUS
Mud puppy

Classification Order Caudata, Family Proteidae.
Distribution Eastern North America, from southeastern Manitoba and southern Quebec south to Georgia and Louisiana.
Identification Both the young and adults of this species have large feathery gills, reddish-brown in color, on the sides of the head. The head and body are fairly elongated and the eyes are small. The legs are short and stocky, each with four toed feet. The tail is highly compressed. The body is generally gray or rusty brown, with a number of blackish or bluish circular spots on the back. Total length: 8–17 in (20–43 cm).
Habitat Lakes, rivers, and streams.
Biology The mud puppy retains its gills and many of its larval features throughout life. By day it remains hidden among submerged rocks or water vegetation, and at night hunts for food, consisting of crayfish, insects, and small fish. During the breeding season the female lays 30–190 eggs, attaching them separately to the undersides of stones on the bottom. The larvae mature in 4–6 years.

21 PROTEUS ANGUINUS
Olm

Classification Order Caudata, Family Proteidae.
Distribution Northeastern Italy and coastal regions of Yugoslavia, from Istria to Montenegro.
Identification This amphibian has an elongated head with small eyes concealed by the skin. There are reddish feathery gills on either side of the neck. The tail is very compressed. The forefeet have three toes, the back legs two. The body is uniformly white. Total length: 8–12 in (20–30 cm).
Habitat Underground waters of limestone caves.
Biology The olm is an amphibian completely adapted to life in caves. It feeds on small crustaceans and molluscs from the bottom of underground streams. Breeding biology in nature is largely unknown. Observations in captivity have shown there is an elaborate courtship ritual. The female lays 10–70 eggs, fixing them to the underside of a submerged rock. Or, the eggs may be retained in her body where only one or two of them are nourished by the others which break down. The mother then gives birth to well-developed larvae.

---

22 CYNOPS PYRRHOGASTER
Japanese fire-bellied newt

Classification Order Caudata, Family Salamandridae.
Distribution Japanese islands of Honshu, Shikoku, and Kyushu.
Identification The head is rectangular with large eyes and two quite prominent parotoid glands on top. At the base of the neck, on each side, there is a large, conspicuous lobate gland. The body of the male is quadrangular and that of the female cylindrical. The tail is laterally compressed with a crest above and below. The back is blackish or brownish, and the underparts are bright red with a number of irregularly arranged black spots. Spawning males have a filament at the tip of the tail. Total length: 3½–5 in (9–12 cm).
Habitat Ponds, lagoons, ditches, streams.
Biology This newt is found in stagnant or slow-moving waters, and only leaves them to spend time on land during the warmer months. It feeds on small arthropods. In the breeding season, from April to June, the male vibrates his tail in front of the female and eventually deposits a spermatophore. This is picked up by the cloacal lips of his partner, who then lays up to 200 eggs, attaching them separately to aquatic plants.

23 EUPROCTUS MONTANUS
Corsican brook salamander

Classification   Order Caudata, Family Salamandridae.
Distribution   Corsica.
Identification   This salamander has a relatively long, flat head with small eyes and distinct parotoid glands. The tail is laterally compressed and has no crest either above or below. The upper parts are uniformly brown or olive, or with a few greenish streaks. There is a prominent projection, with a convex edge, on the outer surface of the male's hind feet. Total length: 3¼–4½ in (8–11.5 cm).
Habitat   Mountain brooks and streams.
Biology   As a rule, metamorphosed individuals estivate and hibernate on land, under rocks or bark, but in some areas they may be encountered in streams at any time of the year. Breeding takes place in slow-running water. The form of mating is rather unusual: the male secures the rear part of the female's body with his tail, ejects a spermatophore, and transfers it with his hind feet to her cloaca. After coupling, the female lays 20–60 eggs, attaching them separately to the underside of submerged stones.

---

24 NOTOPHTHALMUS VIRIDESCENS
Eastern newt

Classification   Order Caudata, Family Salamandridae.
Distribution   Eastern North America, from Ontario and Nova Scotia south to Florida and Texas.
Identification   In adults which lead an aquatic life, the back is olive or yellow-brown, peppered with numerous black spots. Northern examples, ("red spotted newts"), have two lateral rows of black-bordered red spots. Individuals which live exclusively on land for two or three years are bright orange-red after metamorphosis. Spawning males have a swollen cloacal region and black horny structures on the inside of the back legs and toes tips. Total length: 1½–3¼ in (4–8 cm).
Habitat   Lakes, ponds, stream backwaters with dense aquatic vegetation, and damp woodlands.
Biology   Aquatic adults are found in stagnant or slow-flowing water and are voracious feeders. They eat invertebrates and amphibian eggs and larvae. Breeding takes place in winter and early spring when each female lays 200–400 eggs, attaching them separately to submerged vegetation. The eggs hatch in 1–2 months and the larvae metamorphose at the end of summer. Newts secrete a toxic skin secretion and are thus protected from fish and other predators.

25 PARAMESOTRITON CHINENSIS
Chinese warty newt

Classification   Order Caudata, Family Salamandridae.
Distribution   Northeastern coast of China, Ningpo Island.
Identification   This newt has a flat head with large eyes and a short, square snout. The parotoid glands are small. The body bears a fairly prominent vertebral crest and a barely visible line of costal tubercles on either side. The tail is laterally compressed, with a crest above and below. The upper parts are dark brown or olive, the underparts black or bluish, with many small reddish-orange spots. The cloaca of the spawning male is very swollen and there is a white band on either side of the tail. Total length: 4½–6 in (11–15 cm).
Habitat   Fast-moving mountain streams with clear, well-oxygenated water.
Biology   The Chinese newt lives on the rocky or stony beds of mountain streams. It is active mainly at night and feeds on small crustaceans and insects. Breeding occurs from November to April, and the males court the females with characteristic undulating movements of the tail. The eggs are attached separately to water plants.

26 PLEURODELES WALTL
Spanish ribbed newt

Classification   Order Caudata, Family Salamandridae.
Distribution   Southwest Iberian peninsula and northwestern Morocco.
Identification   The head is very flat with small eyes. On either side of the body is a row of yellow or orange warty protuberances which coincide with rib tips. The tail is laterally compressed, with a crest above and below. The back is yellowish or olive, with many brown spots. The underparts are yellow or whitish, with numerous black streaks. During the breeding season the males develop nuptial pads on the inside of the forelegs. Total length: 5¼–12 in (13–30 cm).
Habitat   Ponds, slow-moving rivers, reservoirs, ditches.
Biology   The "sharp-ribbed" newt leads an almost wholly aquatic life and leaves the water only in periods of drought when pools dry up. It is active mainly at night and is extremely voracious. Mating and egg-laying occur from September to June. The male, after wriggling beneath the female's body, uses his feet to manipulate her on to his back, and then deposits a spermatophore which is collected by her cloacal lips. She lays 700–800 eggs, attaching them to water plants.

27   SALAMANDRA ATRA
Alpine salamander

Classification   Order Caudata, Family Salamandridae.
Distribution   Alps of southern Bavaria, Austria; mountain regions of France, Switzerland, Yugoslavia, and northern Albania.
Identification   The species has a flat head with large, protruding eyes. The parotoid glands are very prominent. The body is flattened with clearly visible costal grooves. The tail is short and cylindrical. The body color is normally a uniform black, but some populations possess large bright yellow spots. The male is more slender than the female and is recognizable, too, by his swollen cloacal region. Total length: 4½–6½ in (11–16 cm).
Habitat   Wooded slopes, coniferous mountain forests, and alpine meadows.
Biology   The alpine (black) salamander has markedly terrestrial habits and spends its entire life without ever entering the water. It is active mainly at dusk or by night, especially after heavy rain. The breeding season is from May to July. The species is viviparous; gestation lasts 1–3 years and each female gives birth to 2 young which are exactly like the adults but barely 2 in (5 cm) long. They are sexually mature at 3–4 years.

---

28   SALAMANDRA SALAMANDRA
Fire salamander

Classification   Order Caudata, Family Salamandridae.
Distribution   Western, central, and southern Europe, northwest Africa and southwestern Asia.
Identification   The head is broad and flat with large, prominent eyes. The parotoid glands are always very distinct. The coloration is very striking – shiny black with yellow or reddish spots which differ considerably in shape and arrangement according to locality. The male's cloacal region is swollen. Total length: 6–12¾ in (15–32 cm).
Habitat   Forests traversed by streams, woods near pools and springs.
Biology   The fire salamander is found among the leaf litter of woodland areas and spends the day inside underground burrows or beneath rotting trunks. It is active almost only at night, particularly after heavy showers, when it surfaces to look for food, consisting mainly of insects and earthworms. It can withstand cold conditions and hibernates only in the harshest months of the year. Mating occurs on land either in spring or autumn. The female gives birth in shallow water to as many as 70 larvae, which metamorphose within 2–3 months. They are sexually mature at 4 years.

29 SALAMANDRINA TERDIGITATA
Spectacled salamander

Classification   Order Caudata, Family Salamandridae.
Distribution   Italian peninsula, from Liguria to Campania.
Identification   This species has a distinctive triangular reddish or yellow mark between the eyes. The tail is longer than the rest of the body and the hind feet each have four toes. The back is black or brownish. The throat and belly are white with a number of black spots, and the underside of the tail, legs and cloacal region are bright red. Total length: 2¾–4½ in (7–11 cm).
Habitat   Wooded mountainsides traversed by clear, cool streams.
Biology   The spectacled salamander is active only at night or in cool, cloudy weather, when it comes out to hunt small arthropods, caught with its long, toad-like tongue. In hot, dry weather it remains deeply entrenched in the soil. Mating occurs on land, and in late winter or spring; females enter the water to lay 30–80 eggs on the undersides of submerged stones. The larval phase lasts about 2 months. If disturbed, specimens feign death by curling up and exposing red underside.

30 TARICHA TOROSA
California newt

Classification   Order Caudata, Family Salamandridae.
Distribution   Coastal and Sierra Nevada ranges of California.
Identification   This species has large, protruding eyes with light-colored lower lids. The upper parts are uniformly reddish-brown while the underside is yellowish or orange. The skin is normally granular but becomes smooth in spawning males. The latter have a swollen cloacal region, blackish horny toe tips, and a laterally compressed tail. Total length: 5–7¾ in (13–20 cm).
Habitat   Streams, lakes, and ponds and surrounding conifer and deciduous forests.
Biology   Breeding takes place in winter and spring. After fertilization, the female lays 12–20 eggs in spherical masses. These hatch in 1–2 months and the larvae metamorphose in autumn or following spring. Transformed individuals remain on land and return to water at breeding time. During the rainy season they may be seen during the day searching for invertebrate prey. When disturbed, this newt assumes a curious defensive stance, arching its body and raising its head and tail to display the bright warning colors on its underside.

31 TRITURUS ALPESTRIS
Alpine newt

Classification   Order Caudata, Family Salamandridae.
Distribution   Western, central and southeastern Europe.
Identification   Adult males of this species have an exceptionally brilliant courtship livery. In the breeding season they have a yellow and black, smooth-edged crest along the back, bluish upper parts and a silvery band, with black spots, bordered by a sky-blue stripe, on the flanks. The female has no crest along the vertebral column. The underparts are yellow or orange in both sexes. The cloaca is hemispherical and swollen in the male, oval and less prominent in the female. Total length: 3½–4¾ in (9–12 cm).
Habitat   Lakes, ponds, swamps, slow-moving streams.
Biology   The alpine newt is found at the edge of shallows or deep open water far from the bank. Breeding season occurs in late winter through spring depending on location and elevation. The male, after a brief pursuit, positions himself in front of the female and undulates his tail. When courtship is concluded, he deposits a spermatophore that is picked up by the female's cloacal lips. The eggs are attached separately to aquatic plants. The larval phase usually lasts 3–4 months but is sometimes protracted for 1–2 years.

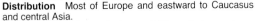

32 TRITURUS CRISTATUS
Crested newt, warty newt

Classification   Order Caudata, Family Salamandridae.
Distribution   Most of Europe and eastward to Caucasus and central Asia.
Identification   The male in courtship garb has a large toothed crest along the back and a mother-of-pearl stripe on the sides of the tail. The female has no vertebral crest but does have tail ridges, at least during the breeding period. The back is dark green or brown, with large circular black marks and a fine sprinkling of white spots on the flanks. The underparts are yellow or orange with numerous black spots. Total length: 5–7 in (13–18 cm).
Habitat   Deep weedy pools, ponds, slow-moving streams and adjacent woodlands.
Biology   In the breeding season, which may be in winter or spring, depending on climate and latitude, the "warty newt" frequents quiet waters with plenty of submerged plants. The courtship ritual performed by the male is similar to that of other newts and culminates with the deposition of a bundle of sperm which is retrieved by his partner's cloacal lips. The eggs are attached separately to aquatic plants.

33 TRITURUS MARMORATUS
Marbled newt

Classification   Order Caudata, Family Salamandridae.
Distribution   Southern and western France and Iberia.
Identification   The breeding male has a high, smooth-edged dorsal crest, with dark vertical bars, and a tail which is adorned on either side by a silvery band. The female has no crest and displays a longitudinal orange stripe along the back. The upper parts are pale green or olive-yellow, with numerous black spots. The underparts may be brown, gray or blackish with a number of white spots. The male's cloaca is hemispherical and swollen, the female's oval and inconspicuous. Total length: 4¾–6¼ in (12–16 cm).
Habitat   Ponds, ditches, temporary and permanent pools and nearby woodlands and heathlands.
Biology   The marbled newt is found in pools and ponds only during the breeding season, from February to April. In summer and autumn, the adults lead a mainly terrestrial life and are active principally at night, after heavy rain. Following courtship and fertilization, the female lays 200–300 eggs, attaching them singly to aquatic plants. The larval phase lasts 3–4 months and the young undergo metamorphosis in late summer or autumn.

---

34 TRITURUS VULGARIS
Smooth newt

Classification   Order Caudata, Family Salamandridae.
Distribution   Most of Europe and western Asia.
Identification   Adults of the species have several longitudinal stripes on the head, at least one of which (that passing through the eye) is always conspicuous. The male in courtship condition has a smooth or undulating crest along the back, fringes on hind toes, and a tail that gradually narrows into an apical filament about ¼ in (5–8 mm) long. The female never has a dorsal crest, nor fringes on the toes. The upper parts are brown or olive-yellow, with numerous rounded black spots. The center of the abdominal region is orange while the sides of the belly are white. Total length: 2¾–4½ in (7–11 cm).
Habitat   Ponds, swamps, lakes, ditches, streams, and adjacent wooded and open lands.
Biology   The smooth newt is the most terrestrial of the European newts. This species moves – males first – to breeding waters according to local climate, from February to May. The female lays 200–400 eggs, attaching them with the hind legs to water plants. The larval phase lasts about 3 months.

35 TYLOTRITON VERRUCOSUS
Emperor newt, crocodile newt

Classification Order Caudata, Family Salamandridae.
Distribution Yunnan (China), northern Burma, northern India, northern Thailand, and northern Vietnam.
Identification This newt has a fairly flat, triangular head, on top of which is a prominent V-shaped bony crest. There is also a bony crest down the center of the back. On either side of the back is a distinct longitudinal row of large glandular tubercles. The bony crests on head and back, the two lines of tubercles, the limbs and the tail are all bright yellow or orange, while the rest of the upper parts are black or brown. Total length: 5½–7½ in (14–19 cm).
Habitat Damp forests in mountain regions.
Biology The "crocodile newt" is found in the leaf litter of montane forests and is active mainly at night. Reproduction, which begins in March and extends throughout the rainy season, takes place in marshes and rice paddies. After mating, a ritual similar to that of the Spanish ribbed newt (Plate 26), the female lays 50–100 eggs, attaching them separately to aquatic vegetation. The larvae metamorphose in a year or so, when they are 1½ in (4 cm) long.

36 PSEUDOBRANCHUS STRIATUS
Dwarf siren

Classification Order Caudata, Family Sirenidae.
Distribution Southeastern United States, South Carolina south to Florida.
Identification This amphibian has a very slender eel-like body. The eyes are tiny, with no lids. In both the larvae and adults, there are reddish-brown gill tufts on the sides of the head. The forelegs are short and delicate, with three small toes, while the hind feet are absent. The tail is finned, tip compressed. The back is brown or grayish. Along the flanks are two longitudinal stripes, yellowish, gray or white, stretching from head to tail. Total length: 4–9⅞ in (10–25 cm). (9⅞ in = record size.)
Habitat Swamps, ditches, weedy ponds.
Biology The dwarf siren spends its life among the roots of aquatic plants or in debris at the water's bottom. This secretive amphibian feeds on small crustaceans and insects. During long periods of drought, the siren encases itself in mud beneath the pond bottom. It can survive for a couple of months inside this cocoon. The adults breed in spring and females lay their eggs singly on roots of aquatic plants.

37 SIREN LACERTINA
Greater siren

Classification Order Caudata, Family Sirenidae.
Distribution Southeastern United States along coastal plain.
Identification The species has a long eel-like body. The tail is compressed and finned with tip rounded. The very small, short forelegs have four toes, while the hind legs are absent. The tiny eyes have no lids. There are prominent tufts of external gills on the sides of the head. The upper parts are gray or olive with irregularly arranged dark spots. The flanks are lighter with greenish-yellow markings. Total length: 20–38½ in (50–98 cm). (38½ in = record size.)
Habitat Weedy waters with muddy bottoms.
Biology This large amphibian spends the day concealed among submerged vegetation under debris, or burrowed in mud. If disturbed, it can escape rapidly by swimming with powerful undulations of the body. It feeds on various aquatic invertebrates. Like the dwarf siren, it gets through very dry spells inside a cocoon of mud in a burrow at the bottom of the pool. Reproduction takes place in February and March. The eggs are attached singly to water plants and the larvae hatch April to May.

38 ASCAPHUS TRUEI
Tailed frog

Classification Order Anura, Family Ascaphidae.
Distribution Coastal northwestern United States, southwestern British Columbia, scattered populations eastward into Montana and Idaho.
Identification This species has a broad, flat head, large eyes with vertical pupils, and a fairly thickset body. The male has no vocal sac, and the pear-shaped tail-like structure (really an exterior cloaca) serves as a copulatory organ. The skin is covered with tubercles and tiny warts; it is olive-green to black with numerous dark spots. Total length: 1–2 in (2.5–5 cm).
Habitat Clear, fast-moving streams and mountain rivers and adjacent damp forests.
Biology The tailed frog is found only in cold, well-oxygenated water that flows through the woods and forests of mountain zones. It spends the day hidden under submerged stones and emerges from its shelter at dusk and during the night to feed on small crustaceans and insect adults and larvae. Unlike reproduction in all other living frogs, fertilization is internal. After mating, and at intervals of 2 years, females lay 30–50 eggs on the downstream underside of rocks. The larval phase lasts 1–3 years.

39 BUFO BUFO
Eurasian common toad

Classification   Order Anura, Family Bufonidae.
Distribution   Europe, northwest Africa, and Asia to Japan.
Identification   The head is wider than it is long, with large protruding eyes and horizontal pupils. The parotoid glands are oval and very prominent. The skin is tough, covered with tubercles and warts. The back may be brown, grayish or reddish-brown, with various spots and streaks, irregularly arranged. The underside is whitish or gray. Total length: 3¼–6¼ in (8–16 cm).
Habitat   Woods, scrub, open ground, margins of cultivated land, gardens.
Biology   The common toad has markedly terrestrial habits, being found in many fairly dry habitats and often venturing into built-up areas. During the day it remains hidden under rocks or in burrows, but leaves its shelters at night to look for food, mainly insects. In late winter or early spring, adults head for pools and streams to breed. During mating, in which the male mounts the female, grasping her armpits with the forelegs, the female lays long gelatinous strings of 4,000–10,000 eggs.

---

40 BUFO COGNATUS
Great Plains toad

Classification   Order Anura, Family Bufonidae.
Distribution   Central regions of North America, from Alberta and Wisconsin to Mexico.
Identification   This toad has prominent bony crests on the head which extend forward to form a bony hump on the snout. Behind the eyes, these crests make contact with the small, elongated parotoid glands. The body is short and broad, and the skin of the upper parts is covered with small warts. The back is brown or olive-gray, with numerous white-bordered black spots. Total length: 2–4½ in (5–11 cm).
Habitat   Prairies, dry shrubby areas.
Biology   The toad inhabits lands with loose or sandy soils. It spends the day inside burrows dug in the ground and only emerges at night or in rainy weather. During its nocturnal outings it mainly looks for food, hunting insects and other arthropods. If disturbed, it swells up its body, closes its eyes and lowers its head, assuming a characteristic defensive attitude. From April to September, especially after long rainy periods, the adults head for pools where mating and egg-laying take place.

41 BUFO MARINUS
Marine toad

Classification Order Anura, Family Bufonidae.
Distribution North, Central, and South America. Introduced and acclimatized in many countries outside America.
Identification This is one of the largest anurans and certainly the biggest toad. It has a massive head, with distinct bony ridges on the top and sides. The parotoid glands are large and prominent. The body is broad and stocky, and the limbs are extremely sturdy. As in other toads, the skin is covered with warts. The back is brown or brownish-yellow, with a number of irregularly arranged dark spots, while the belly is whitish or yellowish. Total length: 4–9½ in (10–24 cm).
Habitat Diverse habitats from savannas to rainforests, cultivated lands, suburbia.
Biology This toad lives in widely different surroundings. It is active mainly at night, is extremely voracious and feeds on a variety of invertebrates and small vertebrates. Unfortunately this species has been widely introduced as an insect control agent. In new habitats it competes with native species. Milky secretions from its parotoid glands are toxic and can kill any predator that tries to eat this toad.

---

42 BUFO MELANOSTICTUS
Black-spined toad

Classification Order Anura, Family Bufonidae.
Distribution Southeast Asia, from India east to the Philippines and south to the Sunda Islands.
Identification This toad has a broad, flat head with several fairly pronounced bony ridges on top. The large parotoid glands are elongated and elliptical. The forelegs are quite strong, the hind legs thin by comparison. The skin of the upper surface is covered with horny black-tipped tubercles. Two warty tubercles usually present between the parotoids and larger warts often form parallel rows on the back. The back is brown or brownish-yellow, and the underparts are fawn. Total length: 2¾–4½ in (7–11.5 cm).
Habitat Woods, rainforests, around human settlements, gardens.
Biology The toad frequents a wide variety of environments and inhabits many different types of refuges, hunting various insects at night. The breeding season is usually in spring, but in regions with constant and heavy rainfall it may breed all year round. Mating and egg-laying can occur either in stagnant or slow-flowing water.

43 BUFO REGULARIS
Panther toad

Classification Order Anura, Family Bufonidae.
Distribution Africa, south of the Sahara.
Identification The species has a stocky, broad body and short, robust legs. The head is flat, with fairly long parotoid glands. The coloration of the upper parts is extremely variable – brown, yellow or olive, with or without black spots. The belly is white with a few dark streaks. Total length: 3½–5½ in (9–14 cm).
Habitat Forests, savannas, dry bushlands and oases.
Biology This is the most common and widespread toad in Africa, with a large variety of habitats, and one of the few amphibians to frequent the Saharan oases. It is active only at night and spends the day inside burrows dug in the ground. It is highly voracious and feeds mainly on insects. In the breeding season, which may extend from August until January, the adults seek out pools, where chorusing males attract females. Males mount and clasp females, each of whom lays long ribbon-like strings of up to 24,000 eggs, which are abandoned on the bottom or attached to aquatic plants.

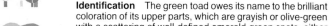

44 BUFO VIRIDIS
Green toad

Classification Order Anura, Family Bufonidae.
Distribution North Africa, central and southern Europe, western and central Asia.
Identification The green toad owes its name to the brilliant coloration of its upper parts, which are grayish or olive-green with a scattering of well-defined emerald-green spots, either isolated or running together. The parotoid glands are narrow and elongated. Total length: 2¾–4 in (7–10 cm).
Habitat Open lowlands, scrub, uncultivated land, gardens, orchards.
Biology This amphibian's life-style does not differ much from that of the common toad and, like the latter, it occupies a great number of habitats and is frequently seen around human habitation. It is mainly nocturnal and when it emerges from its refuge at dusk, it hunts a variety of arthropods. On spring and summer nights the adults visit ponds and the males emit their cricket-like calls. During amplexus, the female lays 5,000–13,000 eggs. The tadpoles metamorphose 1–2 months after hatching.

45 BUFO WOODHOUSEI
Woodhouse's toad

Classification Order Anura, Family Bufonidae.
Distribution United States (apart from extreme west) and northern Mexico.
Identification The species has a fairly short, bluntly rounded snout and large protruding eyes. The bony crests of the head make contact with the parotoid glands, which are prominent and elongated. The upper surfaces are covered with small warts and are gray or greenish-brown with dark spots of varying shape and pattern. A thin white line almost always runs the length of the vertebral line of the body. Total length: 2½–5 in (6–13 cm).
Habitat Sandy ground close to marshes, ponds or temporary pools, and suburbia.
Biology Woodhouse's toad occupies a wide range of natural habitats and is often seen in orchards and gardens on the outskirts or in the center of large towns. It spends the day inside burrows dug in soft soil and emerges only at night to hunt insects. The adults breed in water from March to August.

46 PEDOSTIBES HOSII
Asian climbing toad

Classification Order Anura, Family Bufonidae.
Distribution Extreme southern Thailand, Malaya, Borneo, and Sumatra.
Identification This amphibian has a fairly slender body and long, sturdy hind legs. The eyes are large, with horizontal pupils. The toes of hands and webbed feet have adhesive discs at the tips. The upper parts of males are uniformly brownish-black, with a few indistinct spots on the hind legs. In the females, however, the back may be black, purplish or a bluish-green with bright yellow spots or vermiculations on the flanks. Total length: 2–4 in (5–10 cm).
Habitat Tropical rainforests.
Biology The toad is markedly arboreal and spends most of the day in the foliage of trees and shrubs situated near streams. It is active mainly at night and feeds on various insects. In the breeding season, adults enter the forest streams and the males call in order to attract partners. During amplexus, the females lay long strings of eggs which are attached to aquatic plants.

47 DENDROBATES PUMILIO
Strawberry poison-dart frog

Classification Order Anura, Family Dendrobatidae.
Distribution Nicaragua, Costa Rica, Panama.
Identification This miniature, slim bodied, round snouted frog is brilliant red with sparse black markings. The limbs are marbled dark blue and black. Finger and toe tips are expanded into small adhesive disks. Total length: ¾–1 in (1.8–2.4 cm).
Habitat Tropical rainforests.
Biology This frog is almost always found in the leaf litter and decomposing vegetation of tropical rainforests. Its habits are mostly diurnal and it feeds principally on ants and termites. Its skin contains numerous glands which secrete poisonous substances and is vividly colored as a warning to potential predators. The females lay their eggs among wet leaves. At birth the tadpoles are carried on the backs of the mother to the water-filled rosettes of bromeliads, where they live until metamorphosis.

48 ALYTES OBSTETRICANS
Midwife toad

Classification Order Anura, Family Discoglossidae.
Distribution Western Europe, north to Holland, south to the Alps and Iberia, east to Germany, and Morocco.
Identification This plump anuran has a broad, flat head, and large, protruding eyes with vertical pupils and golden irises. The limbs are short and sturdy, and there are three small tubercles on the underside of the hands. The back is gray or olive-brown, sprinkled with small black warts of varying shapes. The belly is whitish or gray. Total length: 1¼–2 in (3–5 cm).
Habitat Woods, rocky rubble, slides, and gardens.
Biology The midwife toad is a terrestrial amphibian which is active only at night. The breeding season begins after the winter dormancy, when the nights echo to the distinctive owl-like sound of the males calling to the females. Mating takes place on dry land. As the male embraces the female, he gathers the strings of eggs that she lays and winds them around his own hind legs and moves to a damp retreat. After a period that varies from 20 to 50 days, the male, who has carried his bundle of eggs wherever he goes, seeks out a pond and the tadpoles complete their larval development in the water.

49 BOMBINA ORIENTALIS
Oriental fire-bellied toad

Classification   Order Anura, Family Discoglossidae.
Distribution   Southeastern Russia, northeastern China, Korea.
Identification   This toad has a tiny, rounded head and large, protruding eyes with heart-shaped or triangular pupils. The body is fairly short, with sturdy legs. The skin of the upper parts is covered with small black-tipped tubercles. The back is normally bright green with numerous glossy black spots, but it is not unusual to come across individuals that are completely brownish or with spots on the scapular region. The underparts are red or orange-red, marbled with shiny black. Total length: 1¼–2 in (3–5 cm).
Habitat   Ponds, rice paddies, lake shores.
Biology   This toad is found only on the plains of eastern Asia in the vicinity of still water. It feeds mainly on insects and is active both by night and day. During the breeding season, the males give out mournful, nasal croaks which create vibration rings in the water. When mating, the male mounts and clasps the female who lays 40–70 eggs, attaching them to aquatic plants or other submerged objects.

50 BOMBINA VARIEGATA
Yellow-bellied toad

Classification   Order Anura, Family Discoglossidae.
Distribution   Central and southern Europe (except for Iberian Peninsula) southeast to Carpathian Mountains in Russia.
Identification   The upper parts of the body are brown or grayish, a coloration which is in striking contrast to the bright yellow or orange and blue-black marbled belly. The skin of the back is heavily covered with small oval or circular warts. Total length: 1¼–2 in (3–5 cm).
Habitat   Marshes, pools, puddles, ditches.
Biology   Although sometimes found on plains, the yellow-bellied toad usually inhabits hill and mountain regions. It spends the dormant winter period in subterranean burrows, not far from the breeding grounds. The adults are primarily aquatic; mating and egg-laying occur in the water, from May to September. When in danger, without any possibility of flight, this toad takes up a characteristic defensive posture by arching its back, and turning its feet upward to exhibit the bright warning colors of its belly. Its skin secretions are very distasteful to potential predators.

51 DISCOGLOSSUS PICTUS
Painted frog

Classification   Order Anura, Family Discoglossidae.
Distribution   Iberian Peninsula and eastern Pyrenees, northwestern Africa north of the Sahara, Malta, and Sicily.
Identification   In general, the painted frog bears a strong resemblance to the frogs of the *Rana* species, but it has a rounded or heart-shaped pupil and a disk-shaped tongue. This species is highly variable in color and markings: some uniformly gray, olive, or reddish brown, others with dark brown spots or a light stripe on back. Total length: 1½–3¼ in (4–8 cm).
Habitat   Shallows of ponds, streams, marshes, and brackish pools.
Biology   This frog is mainly aquatic but often strays some distance from the pools where it normally lives and breeds. It is active mainly at dusk and by night. Reproduction may take place at various times of the year, but amplexus and egg-laying occur particularly in winter and spring. The female lays 300–1,000 eggs which hatch in 2 to 10 days. The tadpoles transform in 30 to 60 days.

52 HYLA ARBOREA
European treefrog

Classification   Order Anura, Family Hylidae.
Distribution   Central and southern Europe east to Caucasus, Turkey and northwestern coast of Africa.
Identification   This species has fairly slim hind legs, with expanding adhesive pads on the toe tips. The skin is smooth above and granular below. The back is bright green and the belly white. A black or brown stripe extends along the flanks from nostril to groin, forming a small loop in the lumbar region. The males have a vocal sac on the throat. Total length: 1½–2½ in (4–6 cm).
Habitat   Woods, scrub, reedbeds.
Biology   This treefrog leads an arboreal life and rarely comes to the ground. Thanks to the strength of its hind legs, it nimbly climbs trunks and branches, and can make long jumps through the foliage of trees and shrubs. It is active mainly at night, hunting various insects. Breeding occurs in spring, when the adults leave the trees for ponds. Males mount and clasp the females behind the forelegs; each female lays 700–1,000 eggs.

53 HYLA CRUCIFER
Spring peeper

Classification Order Anura, Family Hylidae.
Distribution Eastern North America, from Manitoba to Maritime Provinces south to Florida and Texas.
Identification This frog has brown or olive-gray upper parts, with a large, dark X on the back. As a rule the underparts are pale and unmarked, but individuals from Georgia and Florida may have numerous black spots on the belly. The expanding suction pads on the toes of the feet are larger than those on the fingers of the hands. Total length: ¾–1⅜ in (2–3.5 cm).
Habitat Woodlands close to ponds or swamps.
Biology This frog makes its appearance early in spring. Chorusing males sound like the jingle of bells, a noise regarded as a reliable seasonal guide. It lives mainly in trees, coming to the ground only to hibernate and mate. The breeding season is from November to March in the north, March to June in the south, when the adults frequent stagnant water with plenty of vegetation. As the male clasps her, the female lays clumps of eggs which are attached to water plants. Hatching occurs after a couple of weeks and the larval stage usually lasts about 3 months.

54 HYLA MERIDIONALIS
Mediterranean treefrog

Classification Order Anura, Family Hylidae.
Distribution Northwestern Africa, Canary Islands, southwestern Europe including Portugal, Spain, southern France, and northwestern Italy.
Identification This species resembles the European treefrog but lacks the dark stripe on the flanks, and the green dorsal color extends onto the sides of the throat. Specimens are normally bright green but some brownish or greenish-yellow individuals are found. The back of the thighs is yellow or orange, or with dark mottling. The males have relatively big vocal sacs. Total length: 1½–2½ in (4–6.5 cm).
Habitat Woods and scrub areas near swamps and slow-flowing streams.
Biology This frog spends the day motionless and well camouflaged from predators among the leaves of bushes and shrubs. At dusk and during the night it is highly active and sometimes descends to the ground to hunt insects and centipedes. In spring the adults mass together in swamps and ponds, where mating and egg-laying take place.

55 HYLA REGILLA
Pacific treefrog

Classification Order Anura, Family Hylidae.
Distribution Western North America, from southern British Columbia and western Montana to southern Baja California.
Identification This frog has a blackish stripe which crosses the eye and the tympanum and extends from the nostril to the arm. The skin is rough. Often there is a distinct, dark triangular mark between the eyes. The color of the back is extremely variable: bright green, grayish-brown or black, often with a number of dark spots. The throat of the male is gray. Total length: ¾–2 in (2–5 cm).
Habitat Grasslands, farm country, and woodlands near water.
Biology The frog occupies a wide variety of habitats and is found both in the lowlands and the mountains, sometimes to a height of 10,000 ft (3,000 m). It is principally a ground-dweller and spends its time in the vegetation around marshes, slow streams, ponds, and lakes where it breeds. Egg-laying occurs, depending on climate and latitude, from November to August.

56 LITORIA CAERULEA
White's treefrog

Classification Order Anura, Family Hylidae.
Distribution New Guinea, northern and eastern Australia; introduced to New Zealand.
Identification This large plump frog is bright green above with a few small, irregularly arranged white spots on the sides. The skin is smooth or grainy on the back, and coarsely granular on the flanks and belly. A prominent fold of skin above the tympanum extends from the back of the eye almost to the arm. The tips of the toes have very broad adhesive disks. Total length: 2–4 in (5–10 cm).
Habitat Woodlands, shrubby areas, stands of trees close to natural or artificial bodies of water.
Biology This species is common in Australia, often encountered around ponds and rainwater tanks, and sometimes in farm buildings. In the wild it spends most of its time in trees and hunts food day and night. Breeding is in summer, the adults massing together in pools and ponds to mate and lay eggs.

57 PSEUDACRIS CLARKI
Spotted chorus frog

Classification   Order Anura, Family Hylidae.
Distribution   Central Kansas south through central Texas.
Identification   This very small, attractively marked gray frog displays bright green, black-bordered spots. These markings are usually arranged in irregular fashion but may be fused to form longitudinal stripes on the back. Both spotted and striped individuals have a conspicuous green triangle between the eyes. The toes have tiny round tips. Total length: ¾–1¼ in (2–3 cm).
Habitat   Grasslands and short-grass prairies.
Biology   The species is found mainly on the ground, hopping about in the grass. It ventures out at dusk and by night, completely inactive by day and during dry periods. The males emit a loud rasping trill which sounds a bit like a saw. In northern parts of the range, adults breed in April and May, while in the extreme southern areas, egg-laying may occur virtually at any time of year.

58 PTERNOHYLA FODIENS
Burrowing treefrog

Classification   Order Anura, Family Hylidae.
Distribution   Southern Arizona and south along Pacific coast of Mexico.
Identification   The top part of the skull has a thick bony helmet, to which the skin of the head is attached. There is a prominent bony crest between the eyes and the nostrils, and a distinct fold of skin at the rear of the head, behind the eyes. The upper parts are brown or yellowish, with black-fringed brown spots. In some individuals these spots merge to form longitudinal stripes. On the lower side of the hind foot there is a large, horny, whitish tubercle. Total length: 1½–2½ in (4–6 cm).
Habitat   Open grasslands and shrub forests.
Biology   The species comes out only at night. It spends the day and hot, dry periods in underground burrows excavated with the hind feet. The males give out a series of loud, low-pitched squawks repeated at 2 to 3 calls per second. Mating and egg-laying take place in temporary ponds which form after heavy summer rains.

59 HYPEROLIUS MARMORATUS
Marbled reed frog

Classification Order Anura, Family Hyperoliidae.
Distribution East Africa, Tanzania and southern Kenya.
Identification The frog has long, slender hind legs and expanded pads on the tips of the toes. The color of the upper parts is extremely variable, with distinct two-colored forms. In northern areas of the range, the back may be light brown, gray or pink, with numerous dark streaks or variously shaped black spots. In the southern zones, however, the young and some of the adult males have a uniformly dark longitudinal band on the back, while the females and some other males display alternate light and dark longitudinal stripes. Total length: ¾–1½ in (2–3.5 cm).
Habitat Open brushlands, swampy plains.
Biology In winter the adults of the species are plentiful in the vicinity of swamps and temporary pools, mating and laying eggs in the water. After the breeding season they become very elusive, becoming almost exclusively nocturnal and spending the day hidden in dense vegetation.

60 KASSINA SENEGALENSIS
Senegal running frog

Classification Order Anura, Family Hyperoliidae.
Distribution Entire savanna region of tropical western, central, eastern, and southern Africa.
Identification The species has a broad, flat head, and large eyes with vertical pupils. The tips of the toes are rounded but never expanded to form adhesive pads. The hind legs are relatively short and thin, and the toes are unwebbed. The back is brown or grayish-white, with three distinct brown longitudinal stripes; one down the middle, extending from the tip of the snout to the hindparts, and two down the sides, from the eye region to the groin. Total length: 1¼–1½ in (3–4 cm).
Habitat Savannas, open grasslands.
Biology This amphibian is nocturnal, spending the day and dry periods in underground burrows. It walks rather than hops, and feeds on various insects. The male's vocal sac becomes greatly expanded while calling. The call is loud and distinctive and resembles an escaping bubble of air or a cork being removed from a bottle. Breeding occurs in winter in swamps or temporary pools.

61 CERATOPHRYS ORNATA
Ornate horned frog

Classification   Order Anura, Family Leptodactylidae.
Distribution   Northern Argentina, Uruguay, and Rio Grande do Sul, Brazil.
Identification   The horned frog has a large, heavy body, short and fairly strong legs, and a high and broad head. The mouth is very big and the eyes, large and protruding, are topped by triangular-shaped ridges with pointed tips. The skin is covered with warts and is bright green, with many large, yellow-bordered, brown or blackish spots. Between these spots, especially on the flanks, the green coloration is often replaced by deep red. Total length: 3½–5 in (9–13 cm).
Habitat   Tropical rainforests.
Biology   These frogs inhabit damp areas with plenty of vegetation. They venture into jungle pools only to mate and lay eggs, spending most of their time concealed under leaves or moss, only the top of the head protruding and the eyes keenly alert to surrounding noises. When an amphibian or small mammal imprudently passes close by, they grab hold immediately, killing the prey with their powerful jaws and then swallowing it.

62 HYLACTOPHRYNE AUGUSTI
Barking frog

Classification   Order Anura, Family Leptodactylidae.
Distribution   Southeastern Arizona and southeastern New Mexico to central Texas and central and western Mexico.
Identification   This frog has a fairly big head and large eyes with horizontal pupils, a short and sturdy toad-like body, and relatively short legs. The skin of the upper parts is smooth. There is a lateral fold of skin on the back of the head that connects the tympanums and a large disk-shaped fold on the belly which probably helps the animal climb and attach itself to vertical rock faces. The back is greenish or reddish-brown, with numerous dark spots of varying shape and pattern. Total length: 2½–3¾ in (6–9.5 cm).
Habitat   Caves, wet rock faces with plenty of cracks.
Biology   The frog lives in holes and rock fissures and is active mainly at night. If disturbed or frightened, it defends itself by swelling up enormously to deter the predator. The vernacular name is derived from the fact that the males give out deep calls similar to the barking of a dog. Mating and egg-laying both occur on land. There is no aquatic larval phase and the eggs hatch as miniature frogs.

63 GASTROPHRYNE CAROLINENSIS
Eastern narrow-mouthed frog

Classification   Order Anura, Family Microhylidae.
Distribution   Southeastern United States.
Identification   The species has a narrow, pointed snout and small eyes with round pupils. Behind the eyes, where the head meets the body, there is a pronounced transverse fold of skin. The body is oval and the skin is smooth. On the inner surface of the foot is a horny tubercle with a sharp edge. The back is grayish or reddish-brown, with various black spots, irregularly arranged. There is a broad lateral band along either flank. Total length: ¾–1½ in (2–4 cm).
Habitat   Moist ground with plenty of plant debris.
Biology   Adults are very efficient diggers and voracious eaters of ants and termites. They spend the day in underground burrows and come to the surface only at night, hopping around very quickly. In rainy spring and summer periods, sexually mature females move to water in response to the lamb-like bleat call of the male. In the course of mating, each female lays 10–90 eggs, which float on the water surface.

---

64 KALOULA PULCHRA
Malayan narrow-mouthed toad

Classification   Order Anura, Family Microhylidae.
Distribution   Southern China southward to Singapore and Borneo, Sulawesi, south India, and Sri Lanka.
Identification   The head is small and broad, the large eyes have horizontal pupils, and the snout is short and rounded. The body is quite plump and the limbs are short and sturdy. The front toe tips are enlarged into blunt adhesive disks. The skin of the back is rough and the color dark brown, with two wide bands, yellow or orange, bordered underneath by a long dark stripe. There is a brownish-yellow mark on the head, between the eyes. Total length: 2–3¼ in (5–8 cm).
Habitat   Forests, fields with soft, wet soil, gardens.
Biology   This frog is found in a wide variety of habitats and is very common in parks and gardens of towns and villages. It is nocturnal and spends the day hidden under stones or vegetation. In rainy periods the adults seek out pools and swamps, from which the males give out their loud calls. The eggs are very small and float as a thin layer on the water's surface.

65 PHRYNOMERUS BIFASCIATUS
Red-banded crevice creeper

Classification Order Anura, Family Microhylidae.
Distribution Southern Africa.
Identification The species has a small head, tiny eyes, and a relatively long body. There is an adhesive disk on the tip of each toe. The dorsal color is black or brown, with a large brick-red stripe which extends on either side of the back from the tip of the snout to the groin. There is a large red spot on the sacral region. The belly is black with some white markings. Total length: 2–3¼ in (5–8 cm).
Habitat Open lowlands around shallow ponds and streams.
Biology This frog, unlike most others, can move its neck and is thus able to rotate its head slightly from side to side. It is an agile climber of rocks and trees, and when disturbed emits a foul-smelling, irritant toxic substance from its skin. It is markedly nocturnal and spends the day and dry periods in burrows dug in the ground or inside termite mounds. After heavy rainfall, the adults breed in pools. The eggs are laid in clumps of 400–1,500, which are attached to submerged plants or left on the bottom.

66 MEGOPHRYS MONTANA
Asian horned frog

Classification Order Anura, Family Pelobatidae.
Distribution Thailand, Malaysian peninsula, Indonesia, and Philippines.
Identification Horned frogs are particularly interesting for the long skin projection on the tip of the snout and for the triangular pointed appendages, similar to horns, on each of the upper eyelids. The large eyes have vertical pupils. Two folds of skin on the back extend from the rear of the head to the groin; and there are two similar folds on the flanks. The upper parts are brownish or reddish-brown. The underparts are creamy. Total length: 2–4¾ in (5–12 cm).
Habitat Tropical rainforests.
Biology This amphibian is very common in virgin forest areas, where it lives in the foliage. It has nocturnal habits and spends the day hidden under plant detritus. It is a skillful and voracious predator, feeding on various invertebrates. Mating and egg-laying take place in forest streams. The tadpoles have a funnel-shaped mouth which is specialized for feeding on microorganisms on the water's surface.

67 PELOBATES FUSCUS
European spadefoot

Classification   Order Anura, Family Pelobatidae.
Distribution   Central Europe, from France north to southern Sweden and south to northern Italy eastward to southern Siberia and northern Caucasus in Russia.
Identification   There is a fairly pronounced hump on the back of the head; and the large protruding eyes have vertical pupils. On the inside of each foot is a crescent-shaped, horny tubercle, with sharp edges. The skin is smooth and the back color ranges from olive-gray to brown or yellowish-white, with black-bordered brown or reddish-brown spots, which in some individuals may merge to form two longitudinal bands. They often smell like garlic. Total length: 1½–3¼ in (4–8 cm).
Habitat   Open or wooded plains with sandy or sandy-clay soils.
Biology   The spadefoot is a typical burrowing species with nocturnal habits. It spends the day and periods of winter and summer dormancy in underground burrows which may be quite deep. In soft soil it can bury itself very rapidly with sideways digging movements of its heels. Breeding, from March to June, occurs in the water of ponds and ditches. In the course of mating, each female lays gelatinous strings of 1,000–3,000 eggs.

---

68 PELOBATES SYRIACUS
Syrian spadefoot

Classification   Order Anura, Family Pelobatidae.
Distribution   Balkans and southwestern Asia.
Identification   Unlike the European spadefoot, the top of the head is flat and not humped. The crescent-shaped horny tubercle on the inside of each foot is somewhat bigger than that of the common species, and the skin of the upper parts is often covered with small, irregular warts. The back is grayish, yellowish, or whitish, with large green or brown spots, often dark-edged. Sometimes the back and, especially, the flanks are sprinkled with reddish spots. Total length: 2–3½ in (5–9 cm).
Habitat   Plains and hills with sandy soil.
Biology   The living habits of this species are similar to those of the common spadefoot. It is active by night and spends the day hidden in burrows dug in the ground with the strong hind limbs. Only during the breeding season, at the beginning of spring, do the adults come out by day, but always on the banks or at the bottom of ponds. Mating takes place in clear, deep water.

69 SCAPHIOPUS COUCHI
Couch's spadefoot

Classification   Order Anura, Family Pelobatidae.
Distribution   Southwestern United States and northern Mexico.
Identification   This species has a rounded body, a large head, flat on top, and big protruding eyes with vertical pupils. The skin is smooth but covered with many small, pale tubercles. There is a large, black, crescent-shaped, horny tubercle on each foot. The back is brown or greenish-yellow, with dark marblings. The belly is almost uniformly white. Total length: 2–3½ in (5–9 cm).
Habitat   Prairies, arid or semi-arid mesquite savanna and creosote bush desert.
Biology   It spends the day and periods of prolonged drought inside burrows dug in the soft soil. During the night it surfaces and hunts for insects. From April to September, especially after heavy rain, the adults abandon their underground lairs and seek out temporary pools for breeding. The tadpoles may hatch 3 days after the eggs are laid and grow extremely fast, so that within 2–3 weeks many have completed their larval development and undergo metamorphosis before pools dry up.

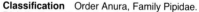

70 PIPA PIPA
Surinam toad

Classification   Order Anura, Family Pipidae.
Distribution   South America, from Ecuador to Guianas and southward to Peru, Bolivia, and Brazil; Trinidad.
Identification   The head is very big, flat and triangular, the eyes are extremely small with rounded pupils, and the nostrils open at the end of two short, narrow tubes at the tip of the snout. The body is quite flat, the forelegs are short and delicate, the hind legs long and sturdy with webbed feet. The skin of the upper parts has many tubercles and is brown or olive-brown. Total length: 4–7 in (10–18 cm).
Habitat   Sluggish rivers and canals with muddy bottoms.
Biology   The Surinam toad leads a strictly aquatic existence, living in the river basins of the South American tropics. The invertebrates that constitute its diet are caught after being detected by special star-shaped tactile organs on the fingertips. In the course of mating, the male fertilizes the eggs as they are released by the female and attaches them to her back. The skin then thickens to enclose them almost completely. Larval development occurs inside the egg and after a 3–4 month incubation, metamorphosed individuals, barely ¾ in (2 cm) long, hatch and immediately lead independent lives.

71 XENOPUS LAEVIS
African clawed frog

Classification   Order Anura, Family Pipidae.
Distribution   Central, eastern and southern Africa; introduced into southern California.
Identification   The head is small and much flattened, the eyes, with rounded pupils, are tiny and turned upward, and the body is quite flat. The forelegs are short and delicate, with long, pointed fingers on the hands, while the hind legs are long and sturdy, and the toes are linked by broad webs. The three inner toes have horny sheaths similar to claws. The skin of the upper parts is smooth, brown or greenish-brown with dark streaks. Total length: 4–5 in (10–13 cm).
Habitat   Lakes, swamps, ponds, slow-flowing rivers.
Biology   The clawed frog is strictly aquatic, particularly common in swamps and ponds with plenty of vegetation. It swims extremely fast and can move equally quickly either backward or forward. It hunts on the surface and on the bottom, feeding on tadpoles, small fish and various invertebrates. These frogs are very prolific and large females may produce 2,000 eggs. Larvae hatch in two days and the tadpoles look like tiny catfish with long barbels on their snouts. Carnivorous adults help keep the population in check.

72 CHIROMANTIS XERAMPELINA
Gray foam-nest treefrog

Classification   Order Anura, Family Rhacophoridae.
Distribution   Southeastern Africa: coastal Kenya and northern Namibia south to Natal.
Identification   The upper part of the body is covered with numerous small tubercles and the fingers are furnished with adhesive disks. The toes of the feet are webbed and the first and second (inner) fingers of the hand oppose the third and fourth fingers to form a grasping hand. The back is gray, usually with some black markings on the head and a dark triangular patch between the eyes. The front part of the belly is white or grayish, while the rear part and the lower surface of the thighs are salmon-pink. Total length: 2–3¼ in (5–8 cm).
Habitat   Forests to savannas.
Biology   This arboreal frog is highly sedentary and active only at night. During the breeding season the adults, which normally live some distance from water, venture to trees that overhang ponds or temporary pools. They build a large white foam nest above the water to accommodate about 150 eggs. The tadpoles, which hatch in 2 days and remain in the nest for another 4–5 days, drop into the pond below and complete their larval growth in the water.

73 POLYPEDATES LEUCOMYSTAX
Asian flying frog

Classification Order Anura, Family Rhacophoridae.
Distribution Sikkim and Assam, India and southern China southward to Indonesia and the Philippines.
Identification The head is large and flat, the eyes big and protruding with horizontal pupils. A rather pronounced fold of skin extends from the rear corner of the eye through the tympanum to the shoulder. There are broad adhesive pads on the toetips. The back may be uniformly olive or reddish-yellow, or gray with various irregular dark patches. On the back of the head, between the eyes, there is almost always a dark W-shaped mark. Total length: 1½–3 in (4–8 cm).
Habitat Woods, rainforests, bamboo thickets.
Biology This is an arboreal species which spends the day hidden among the foliage or in tree cavities. At night it comes out and climbs the branches in search of food, mainly insects. In the breeding season the pair in amplexus builds a foam nest on leaves overhanging water; after fertilization, the eggs are laid in these nests. The newly hatched tadpoles fall into the water and complete their larval development there.

74 PYXICEPHALUS ADSPERSUS
African bullfrog

Classification Order Anura, Family Ranidae.
Distribution Central, eastern, and southern Africa.
Identification This frog has a large, stocky body, a massive head, large protruding eyes and an extremely big mouth. There are three characteristically pointed projections, like teeth, on the jaw, and these can inflict painful wounds on would-be predators. The back and the sides are covered with several lines of prominent skin folds, and are dark green or olive-gray, while the underparts are smooth and cream or yellow. Total length: 3¼–8 in (8–20 cm).
Habitat Open, grassy savannas, bushlands.
Biology The species has burrowing habits and uses its strong hind legs, each with a sharp horny tubercle, to dig deep holes in the ground. The adults are extremely aggressive and, if molested, swell their body up enormously. With their mouth opened wide, they can swallow large frogs, rodents, and small birds. In the rainy season these frogs leave their underground burrows for ponds or temporary pools, where they breed. Each female lays 3,000–4,000 eggs in huge gelatinous bundles.

75 RANA CATESBEIANA
American bullfrog

Classification   Order Anura, Family Ranidae.
Distribution   Southeastern Canada, eastern and central United States, and south to Veracruz, Mexico. Introduced widely into the western United States and elsewhere.
Identification   The head is large and the snout rounded, the eyes big with horizontal pupils, the body heavy and stocky. The tympanum is round; in the female its diameter is equal to that of the eye, in the male it is much bigger. The upper parts are olive-green or brown, rarely black, with dark spots or mottling. The underparts are uniformly whitish, or white with a few black marks. Total length: 3½–8 in (9–20 cm).
Habitat   Lakes, ponds, swamps, ditches.
Biology   The bullfrog is usually seen along the margin of natural or artificial lakes. Active both by day and night, it is extremely voracious and feeds on large flying insects, crustaceans and small fish. At dusk and during summer nights the familiar "jug-o-rum" call of the male can be heard at great distance. In the breeding season females may lay over 20,000 eggs which form a large, wide floating mass, one egg deep, on the surface.

76 RANA DALMATINA
Agile frog

Classification   Order Anura, Family Ranidae.
Distribution   Widely ranging in Europe (except most of Iberia and northern Europe) and Asia Minor.
Identification   The agile frog sports a dark mask and has a sharply pointed snout, a fairly slender body and very long hind legs. Down the back and sides of the body run two prominent ridges of skin. The color is very variable – gray, brown or reddish, with a few or many black spots. The underparts are white or yellowish, often with tiny dark spots on the throat. Total length: 2–3½ in (5–9 cm).
Habitat   Woodlands close to ponds or streams, reed beds fringing swamps, marshes.
Biology   The species is strictly terrestrial, frequenting areas of tree growth and fields on the margins of woods, and active mainly at dusk and during the night. The winter dormancy period is quite short and adults seek out water in which to breed before the cold season is over. In the course of mating, which usually occurs at night and lasts several hours, the females lay 600–2,000 eggs. The eggs hatch in 15–30 days and the tadpoles metamorphose within 2–3 months.

77 RANA ESCULENTA
Edible frog

Classification Order Anura, Family Ranidae.
Distribution Central Europe.
Identification The edible frog is of hybrid origin, derived from the pool frog (*Rana lessonae*) and the marsh frog (*R. ridibunda*). In morphology and coloration it shares features with both parental species. The color is grass-green or brown with dark spots, sometimes fused to form longitudinal bands, as in *R. lessonae*. The males' vocal sacs may be white, as in *R. lessonae* or, more rarely, gray as in *R. ridibunda*. Total length: 3½–4¾ in (9–12 cm).
Habitat Lakes, swamps, ponds, permanent and temporary pools.
Biology The edible frog is capable of mating with either of its parental species which may share its habitat. But the progeny of such couplings, by virtue of a peculiar reproductive mechanism, produce more edible frogs. Collectively known as "green frogs," they are noisy, relatively aquatic, and gregarious and contrast with the quieter, more terrestrial "brown frogs" like *R. dalmatina* and *R. temporaria*.

78 RANA GRYLIO
Pig frog

Classification Order Anura, Family Ranidae.
Distribution Southeastern United States, from South Carolina to Texas.
Identification This big frog looks much like a bullfrog, with a large round tympanum, the male's greater in diameter than the eye, the female's equal in diameter. Unlike the bullfrog, however, the pig frog has a narrow pointed snout, and fully webbed hind feet. The upper parts are olive-gray or dark brown, with numerous irregular black spots, while the belly is white or yellowish. The undersides of the thighs bear dark streaks. Total length: 3–6⅜ in (8–16 cm).
Habitat Lake shores, ponds, marshes.
Biology The species is often seen floating among a cover of floating or emergent vegetation. Active mainly by night, it is extremely voracious, feeding on insects and crustaceans. Mating and egg-laying occur from March to September, when the males emit loud pig-like grunts. The tadpoles may grow to a length of 5 in (13 cm) and transform in 2 years.

79 RANA PIPIENS
Northern leopard frog

Classification Order Anura, Family Ranidae.
Distribution North America (except for southeastern United States and Pacific coastal regions).
Identification The leopard frog has a bluntly pointed snout and two pale-colored longitudinal skin ridges running from its eyes to the groin. The upper parts are grass-green or brown, with many light-bordered dark spots. There is a prominent white or yellow stripe on the upper jaw. Total length: 2–5 in (5–13 cm).
Habitat Ponds, swamps, marshes, flooded fields.
Biology The species frequents still waters, especially in spring, when breeding occurs. In summer it abandons the water to live in fields and wet meadows. It is active mainly at night and feeds on various insects. The males emit low, guttural snores from the water during spawning. The eggs, in compact bundles, are attached to submerged plants or sink to the bottom. The larval phase lasts about 3 months and the tadpoles undergo metamorphosis at the beginning of autumn.

80 RANA TEMPORARIA
European common frog

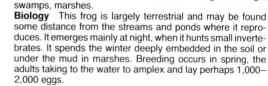

Classification Order Anura, Family Ranidae.
Distribution Europe east to the Urals (except for most of Iberia, Italy, and the southern Balkans).
Identification The common frog has a bluntly rounded snout and large eyes with horizontal pupils. There are two longitudinal folds of skin down the back and flanks. The dorsal color is rather variable, ranging from brown or gray to reddish or greenish-yellow, usually with dark brown spots or streaks. The abdomen is white or yellowish, sometimes with gray or brownish streaks. Total length: 2½–4 in (6–10 cm).
Habitat Woodlands close to streams or lagoons, bogs, swamps, marshes.
Biology This frog is largely terrestrial and may be found some distance from the streams and ponds where it reproduces. It emerges mainly at night, when it hunts small invertebrates. It spends the winter deeply embedded in the soil or under the mud in marshes. Breeding occurs in spring, the adults taking to the water to amplex and lay perhaps 1,000–2,000 eggs.

INTRODUCTION

The first true land tetrapods, very probably stemming from a group of amphibious Labyrinthodontia (Anthracosauria), appeared on earth more than 300 million years ago, in the early Upper Carboniferous period, and originated a new class of vertebrates, the reptiles. The most extraordinary evolutionary advance of these animals was the amniotic egg. This new type of egg rendered the aquatic larval phase superfluous, inasmuch as it held an abundant reserve of nutritive substances and, above all, contained a special fluid-filled sac which represented a facsimile in miniature of the watery environment in which the amphibian embryo developed. The reptile's egg, with its tough, protective shell, was a remarkable, self-sufficient structure which, unlike that of amphibians, could be laid on land. Yet despite its enormous importance, the amniotic egg was not the only successful experiment in the evolution of the reptiles. Life on dry land made it essential for these vertebrates to reduce their water loss through transpiration. Consequently, and in association with the principal role assumed by the lungs in breathing, the reptile's skin lost its function as an organ designed for gaseous exchanges, and became a thickened, cornified structure suitable for protecting the animal from shocks and risks of dehydration. The organs regulating hydric equilibrium also underwent profound modifications, culminating in the evolution of a physiological mechanism capable of reabsorbing metabolic water through the cloaca and of elminating a creamy urine rich in uric acid. Another structural innovation was the relatively complete ossification of the skeleton which strengthened the limbs that on dry land had to support the body and allow rapid and purposeful locomotion.

Thanks to the amniotic egg, pulmonary respiration, and strengthening of the skeleton and integument, representatives of the ancestral stock of reptiles broke free, in large measure, from the liquid element and quite soon conquered almost all the available habitats to be found on dry land. From these primitive reptiles, still closely related to the Anthracosauria, two major branches stemmed during the Early Carboniferous: the Anapsida (reptiles with closed skulls) including the "stem reptiles" of the order Cotylosauria, and the Synapsida (reptiles with a single temporal opening in the skull), which were the progenitors of the mammals.

The cotylosaur branch was undoubtedly the most important in the history of reptiles, including as it did the ancestors of the diapsid reptiles (Lepidosauria and Archosauria), whose skulls had two temporal openings), an upper and a lower, behind the eye, and the euryapsid reptiles (Ichthyopterygia and Euryapsida), with a single, upper temporal fossa. Both the diapsids and euryapsids reached their evolutionary peak during the Mesozoic, which lasted some 160 million years and was known, because of its enormous variety of forms, as the "age of reptiles." When this period ended, most of the principal groups of reptiles disappeared. Of nearly 20 orders known to have existed during the Mesozoic era, only four (the Chelonia, Squamata,

Seymouria bayloriensi, an anthracosaurian amphibian which lived in the Lower Permian era. The anthracosaurs have long been considered the ancestors of the reptiles but the discovery of fossilized aquatic larvae confuses the issue.

Rhynchocephalia and Crocodylia)—those that still populate the earth today—survived the geological and climatic vicissitudes of the period spanning the end of the Mesozoic and the beginning of the Cenozoic era.

THE SUCCESSFUL COLONIZATION OF DRY LAND

The amniotic egg. A reptile's egg, as already mentioned, is laid on land and is provided with a leathery or hard shell constituted in varying degrees of calcium carbonate. Some Squamata bear their young live; here the shell is reduced and the chorionic, allantoic and yolk sac membranes may form a type of placenta. The embryo is situated in the center of the egg and is wrapped by a membrane (amnion) which forms a sac filled with liquid (amniotic sac) which protects the embryo itself from drying out and from shocks. The principal food reserves of the egg are contained in the yolk sac which is connected to the embryo by the umbilical cord. The yolk sac is covered by a network of blood vessels which absorb the food in the sac itself and convey it to the abdominal region of the embryo, which is thus able to feed itself. Both the amniotic and yolk sacs are enclosed in the allantois, a membrane designed to collect the waste products of embryonic metabolism and to regulate the gaseous exchanges between the embryo and the outside environment. The allantois is in turn surrounded by the chorion, a thin protective covering which also functions as

Principal types of skull structure in reptiles. 1) Anapsid-type skull (without temporal openings); 2) Diapsid-type skull (two temporal openings); 3) Euryapsid-type skull (one upper temporal opening); 4) Synpsid-type skull (one lateral temporal opening).

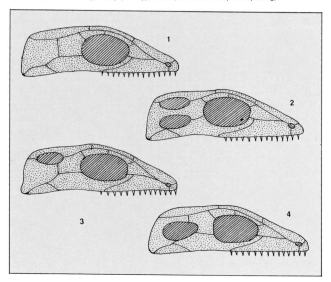

a breathing organ, absorbing the oxygen which penetrates the pores of the shell.

The integument and skeleton. Because most reptiles live on land they must have an effective method of reducing fluid loss. Thus the reptilian body is covered with a relatively impermeable skin. This is arranged in a series of thickenings known as scales (or if enlarged, as plates or scutes). The scales are covered by the horny (keratinized) outer layer of the epidermis, and may be separated by gaps, or juxtaposed or overlapping; the arrangement varies from one species to another. In Chelonia (turtles, tortoises), Crocodylia (crocodiles, alligators, etc.) and some Sauria (lizards) the scales may contain bony dermal plates (osteoderms) which give added protection. The two parts of the chelonian shell (carapace above and plastron below) are double layered, the outer layer being composed of horny plates and the inner one of bony plates. Most of the ribs and trunk vertebrae are typically fused with or attached to the inner surfaces of the bony plates.

Being formed of dead cells, the keratinized layer of the epidermis is incapable of growing and is periodically replaced through the activity of deeper layers of cells. This process is called the shedding or the slough, and it is brought about by the germinative layer of the epidermis which produces cells that come to the surface and cornify. In reptiles the cutaneous glands are as a rule few in number and localized. On the other hand, there are many cells which contain

The drawing below shows the orders or suborders in which all living reptiles are grouped.

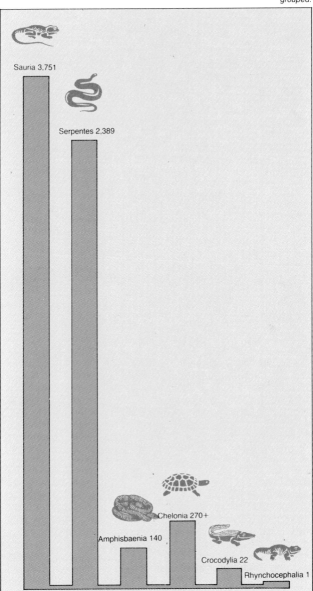

Sauria 3,751

Serpentes 2,389

Amphisbaenia 140

Chelonia 270+

Crocodylia 22

Rhynchocephalia 1

pigment granules (chromatophores): the yellow chromatophores (xanthophores) are situated immediately under the epidermis, while those containing guanine crystals (iridophores) and the black chromatophores (melanophores) are deeper in the dermis. The colors of reptiles, which may be fixed but which in some cases (e.g. chameleons and certain iguanids of the genus *Anolis*) are capable of considerable change, depend on the nature and arrangement of these specialized cells.

The skeleton of reptiles is made up mainly of bony elements and constitutes a stiff supporting system which renders them more adaptable than their predecessors, the amphibians, to life on dry land. To consider first the skull structure of living reptiles: in the turtles the outer wall of the temporal part of the skull, behind the orbits, has no openings or fossae (the anapsid skull condition), though there may be a deep notch at the back. In the skull of crocodilians and the tuatara there are two temporal openings (diapsid skull); the upper fossa is at the top of the skull on each side and the lower one at each side of the "cheek" region. The Squamata have a modified type of diapsid skull; in lizards the bony bar forming the inferior boundary to the lower fossa has disappeared, and only the upper bar is left, at least in typical species. In snakes both of the temporal bars have been lost. Owing to the loss of the lower bar the quadrate bone, which articulates with the lower jaw, becomes relatively free, increasing the mobility of the jaws; this feature is exceptionally well developed in snakes.

The crocodilians and the majority of lizards and snakes have a spinal column formed of procoelous vertebrae while the tuatara and lizards belonging to the family Gekkonidae have amphicoelous vertebrae. The total number of vertebrae varies from species to species and in some snakes may exceed 400. Most living reptiles possess four limbs and have a spinal column consisting of cervical, dorso-lumbar, sacral, and caudal regions. The main exceptions are the snakes, which not only lack the four limbs but also the scapular girdle and the sternum (the pelvic girdle is generally absent; in some primitive forms it is vestigial); the worm-lizards, which either have no limbs (Amphisbaenidae and Trogonophidae) or only a front pair (Bipedidae); and certain lizard species, which exhibit all degrees of limb reduction down to complete loss of the external limbs, as in the slow-worm (*Anguis*).

The bodily size of reptiles, like the shape and individual features, is extremely variable. The giants of the group are today the salt water crocodile (*Crocodilus porosus*), the anaconda (*Eunectes murinus*), and certain pythons, all of which reach and, exceptionally exceed, a length of 20 ft (6.1 m). The smallest representatives of the class are certain lizards in the family Gekkonidae, which do not grow to more than 1½ in (4 cm).

The nervous system and the sensory organs. The nervous system of reptiles is markedly more developed and complex than that of amphibians. The cerebral hemispheres are fairly big and are connected to two olfactory bulbs by long stalks. There is a clear division

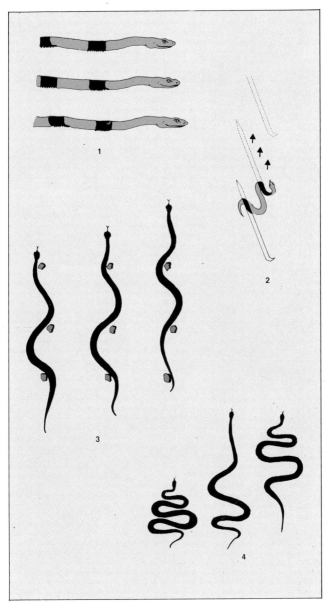

Various phases in lizard locomotion.

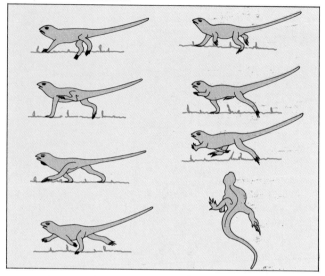

between gray matter, situated near the surface of the vault of the cerebral hemispheres, and white matter. The dorsal region of the diencephalon in the tuatara and some lizards is the site of origin of the parietal, median, or third eye, which, in the live animal, is found inside a small opening in the roof of the skull. This median eye is furnished with a crystalline lens and a retina, but is covered with skin; it may play some part in temperature regulation. The optic lobes of the mid-brain are usually well developed. As in birds and mammals, there are 12 pairs of cranial nerves. The eyes, except in some species such as worm-lizards and those snakes which lead an underground life, are normally large and have a clearly defined retinal structure. In the turtles, crocodilians and the majority of lizards the eye is protected by two mobile lids, an upper and a lower, and by a nictitating membrane which is a transparent fold of skin between the other two lids. In snakes and various members of the gecko and skink families, the lower lid, which is transparent, is fused with the upper one, forming a fixed, transparent structure called the spectacle. Each eye, moreover, is furnished with two large glands which help to keep the cornea constantly moist. As in birds and mammals, the image is typically brought into focus by modification in the shape of the crystalline lens; snakes have a different mechanism.

In the majority of reptiles, comparatively weak sound waves are amplified and transmitted to the inner ear through the structures of the middle ear. This consists of a short outer acoustic meatus, a tympanic membrane and a tympanic cavity. The cavity contains the stapes—a small bone designed to transmit vibrations to the inner ear—and is connected to the pharynx by the Eustachian tube. The snakes and some lizards have no middle ear. These animals are extremely sensitive to vibrations transmitted from the ground to the inner ear through the bones of the skull.

Although some reptiles' tongues are provided with taste buds, the sense of taste does not seem to be highly developed in any of these animals. Smell, on the contrary, is extremely important, as indicated by the large size of the olfactory lobes of the brain. In turtles, the tuatara and Squamata, there is a paired accessory organ of smell, the (vomeronasal) organ of Jacobson, which is especially well developed in many lizards and in snakes. The pit vipers (Crotalinae) have a special heat-sensitive organ, the pit organ, which serves to locate warm-blooded prey and is lodged in a depression of the maxillary bone situated below and behind the nostril. Thanks to this organ, these snakes can perceive, even at night, the direction as well as the weak emanations of heat from the body of an approaching bird or mammal.

Respiration and circulation. The principal breathing organs of reptiles are the lungs. In the squamates and tuatara these organs are sac-shaped with alveolatar walls, whereas in turtles and crocodilians they are divided into compartments, structured much like those of mammals. In many snakes and certain lizards with reduced or absent limbs and a serpentine body, the left lung may be smaller than the right lung or wholly lacking. The trachea, or windpipe, except in snakes, is always supported by cartilaginous rings and is bifurcated in relation to the lungs. Between the trachea and the pharynx is a special structure, the larynx, which is the front part of the windpipe. In lizards belonging to the family Gekkonidae the larynx is equipped with a pair of vocal cords and is thus an organ designed to produce sounds.

Reptiles have a double and incomplete circulatory system. In turtles, tuatara, lizards, and snakes, the heart consists of a single ventricle, which is partially divided by an incomplete septum, and two auricles: the left auricle, which collects oxygenated blood from the lungs, and the right auricle, which receives the blood returning from the various parts of the body. The oxygenated blood therefore mingles, to some extent, with the venous blood. In crocodilians, however, the ventricular septum forms a virtually complete dividing wall and thus there are two proper ventricles, the left and the right. Heart rate of reptiles is extremely variable. Temperature, activity, and digestion of food are contributing factors.

LIFE AND HABITS

Feeding. Some time after its formation, the reptile embryo already begins to feed. In the course of this first phase of life the substances needed for growth are furnished by the abundant store of yolk contained in the egg. After hatching, however, food is no longer brought physiologically to the young and has to be actively sought in the outside environment. Among the turtles, which have no teeth but are provided with a horny, sharp-edged beak which covers the jaws, the land species generally feed on plants or on small invertebrates (mollusks, worms, and insects), while the aquatic forms are omnivorous, eating vegetation and preying upon crustaceans, mollusks, worms, insects, fishes, and larval amphibians.

Crocodilians are likewise aquatic. These carnivores have strong teeth implanted in shallow alveolae in the jaws. Representatives of this order feed chiefly on fish, amphibians, birds, and mammals and other reptiles, and occasionally take crustaceans. They catch their prey in the water or on the shores of lakes and rivers, mangling them with their sharp teeth and swallowing smaller creatures whole. Large prey are dragged to the bottom, drowned, and chunks of flesh are twisted off and bolted.

The teeth of the tuatara, snakes, and many lizards are found in the upper and lower jaws and additionally often on the palatal bones, these being used exclusively for grasping prey. Venomous snakes have specialized teeth for envenomating prey. Opisthoglyphs, or rear-fanged snakes, have grooved teeth on the back of the upper jaw. These snakes cannot inject their prey by merely striking but must chew their victim to introduce the venom. Solenoglyphs (vipers) and proteroglyphs (cobras, etc.) have a pair of grooved or hollow fangs attached to the maxillary bone in the front of the upper jaw. With these teeth the venom secreted by the venom gland ("parotid gland") is injected into the victim's flesh. The venom quickly immobilizes and then kills the prey, and only at this point is it swallowed. On the other hand, those snakes which lack grooved teeth (aglyphous species), often immobilize their victims by constricting them in their coils and, after suffocating them, swallow them head first. Both types of snake, however, are able to expand their mouth enormously in order to swallow—thanks also to the large, extensible esophagus—prey of considerable dimensions.

The lizards also have an extensible esophagus but, in contrast to snakes, their mouth is only moderately expandable and—apart from the Helodermatidae, which includes the only two living venomous lizards—there are no grooved teeth or venom glands. The tongue of these specialized lizards is mobile and bifid, like that of the monitor lizards and snakes. In the snakes there is a notch at the front edge of the jaw so that the tongue can be shot outward even when the mouth is closed. In some lizards the tongue is also used for feeding, helping to convey arthropods and other small prey, or, in the case of vegetarian species, plant stems and leaves, to the mouth. In this context, the most highly specialized hunter of prey is the chameleon, whose very long, club-shaped, sticky tongue is shot out at great speed to trap the victim.

Reproduction. In reptiles, fertilization is an internal process which

*A green lizard (*Lacerta viridis*), snapped while catching an insect.*

culminates, in due course, in the laying of eggs. Male reptiles, with the exception of the tuatara, have copulatory organs. These are situated in pouches at the base of the tail and everted through the cloacal opening during the act of copulation. The turtles and crocodilians have an erectile, protrusible penis, like that of mammals, while the squamates have two grooved, sac-shaped, copulatory organs known as hemipenes. They are often covered with small spines or hooks which probably serve to grip the walls of the female cloaca and which can be evaginated to coincide with the moment of sexual union. Only one hemipenis is actually inserted into the cloaca. In both the penis and hemipenis, sperm flows into a groove on the outer surface of the erect organ during intromission. In the tuatara, which have no copulatory organ, the male transmits sperm to the female simply by the juxtaposition of the respective cloacal apertures. The sperm remain visible in the oviducts for a long time and can in some species fertilize the maturing eggs even after many months. In certain lizards belonging to the families Gekkonidae, Lacertidae and Teiidae, there are no males and thus no fertilization is possible. In these species, consisting of all-female populations, the unfertilized eggs develop nonetheless by means of a process known as parthenogenesis.

The females of most reptiles are oviparous. The eggs are laid beneath stones, in small holes dug in the sand or under trunks and leaves, and are normally left by the mother to their fate. The females of certain lizards and snakes, however, after depositing the eggs, wrap their body around them, thus protecting them throughout incubation.

Different types of dentition in snakes. 1) opisthoglyph (venomous teeth implanted in the rear part of maxillary bone); 2) proteroglyph (venomous teeth implanted in front part of maxillary bone); 3) solenoglyph (venomous teeth implanted in front part of mouth, on a rotatable maxillary bone); 4) aglyph (non-venomous teeth all solid and thus without a groove or canal.

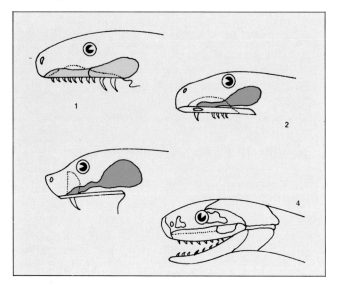

Alligators and crocodiles exhibit true parental care. The females build a mound nest with mud and plant debris or dig a flask-shaped nest hole in a sandbank and, having laid the eggs, remain nearby for the whole incubation period. At hatching, mothers open the nest, carry young to the water, and keep watch over them and protect them from enemies for an extended period of time.

The females of some snakes and lizards do not lay eggs but give birth to babies that are perfectly formed and completely independent. The eggs are retained in the oviducts and the embryos develop entirely within the mother's body. In ovoviviparous species the embryo grows by feeding exclusively on the egg yolk, whereas in viviparous species the food needed for growth is partly or mainly furnished by the mother's blood vessels through a form of placental contact which is established between the walls of the oviduct and the embryonic membranes. The distinction between ovoviviparity and viviparity is not absolute.

Habitats. Reptiles inhabit terrestrial environments almost everywhere on earth. The majority of species are found in tropical and subtropical regions which are climatically best suited to them. Comparatively few reptiles live in temperate or temperate-cold zones: in Europe, for example, one lizard (*Lizard vivipara*) and one viper (*Vipera berus*) range to far northern latitudes, and the situation is similar in America where the most northerly species is the common garter snake (*Thamnophis sirtalis*). There are no reptile species whatsoever in Antarctica, Greenland, Iceland, and the territories around the Polar Circle, quite clearly because of the intense cold that prevails in these areas.

Apart from the air, which in the Mesozoic era was a natural element of the flying archosaurians belonging to the order Pterosauria, there are nowadays no habitats which have not been colonized by reptiles. On dry land these vertebrates can be found on alluvial plains, in temperate woodlands, in tropical forests and even in deserts. They even frequent high mountain regions, as is the case with the Asiatic agamid *Phrynocephalus theobaldi*, which in some parts of the Himalayas is encountered at altitudes above 16,500 ft (5,000 m), or the South American iguanid *Liolaemus multiformis*, which lives in the Andes at heights of 13,500–16,500 ft (4,000–5,000 m). There are reptiles, such as the worm-lizards and the burrowing snakes of the families Typhlopidae and Leptotyphlopidae, which spend much of their lives digging long tunnels underground, and others which live almost exclusively in trees, notably the chameleons, various gecko and iguana species, and, among the snakes, many representatives of the Boidae, Colubridae, Elapidae, and Viperidae. A fairly large number of reptiles, too, populate the waters of lakes, rivers and swamps; the Chelonia, Crocodylia and Squamata all contain freshwater species, particularly in tropical and subtropical zones. But comparatively few frequent saltwater habitats: the only fully marine species of the class are the turtles of the families Cheloniidae and Dermochelyidae and the venomous seasnakes of the family Elapidae ascribed to the subfamily Hydrophiinae.

INTRODUCTION TO CLASSIFICATION

Classification and distribution of reptiles. Many herpetologists divide the class of reptiles into six subclasses: Anapsida, Synapsida, Lepidosauria, Archosauria, Ichthyopterygia, and Euryapsida. Living reptile species, between 6,600 and 6,700, belong to the Anapsida, Lepidosauria and Archosauria. Representatives of the other three subclasses have been extinct for many millions of years. The subclass Anapsida is subdivided into three orders: Cotylosauria (extinct), Mesosauria (extinct) and Chelonia (turtles and tortoises). There are also three subclasses of the Lepidosauria: Eosochia (extinct), Squamata (Sauria, Serpentes, and Amphisbaenia), and Rhynchocephalia (a single living representative in New Zealand). The subclass Archosauria comprises five distinct orders: Thecodontia (extinct), Ornithischia (extinct), Saurischia (extinct), Pterosauria (extinct), and Crocodylia (crocodiles, alligators, and caimans).

The classification of living reptiles followed in this book is that proposed in the *Encyclopedia of Reptiles and Amphibians* by Halliday and Adler (1986). Modifications to this classification essentially affect the families of the Serpentes and are based on the work of Parker and Grandison (1977).

Distribution of reptiles on earth: the distribution area of the lizards and snakes is shown in yellow (the lines indicate that of the marine representatives of the family Elapidae), the distribution of the turtle in red (the lines mark that of the families Cheloniidae and

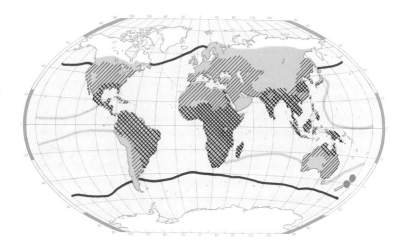

PROTECTION

Principal causes of reptilian rarity and problems of protection.
Reptiles are certainly the vertebrates least known to the public at large and, perhaps for that reason, are widely feared and persecuted, being associated in popular imagination with everything that is most harmful and undesirable. Snakes, lizards, and crocodiles have traditionally aroused sensations of horror and repugnance, and even today these animals are regarded as cruel and dangerous, an attitude which is likely to render their future prospects increasingly uncertain. The general feeling of hostility, compounded by irrational aversion and, almost always, unfounded fear, nowadays represents a menace no less significant than the destruction and pollution of their natural habitats. The alarming and steadily increasing scarcity of many species of reptiles is exemplified by the widespread slaughter of crocodiles and snakes (especially Boidae), mainly for their skins, in all tropical areas, to the ruthless filching of eggs and hunting of adult marine turtles, to the export of large numbers of tortoises, lizards, and snakes destined to a miserable existence in collectors' tanks, and to the continuous and insensate killing of venomous snakes which results in the annual decimation of thousands of absolutely harmless species.

According to the statistics in Rene Honegger's *Red Data Book* (1979) on behalf of the International Union for the Conservation of Nature and Natural Resources, there are today more than 100 species of reptiles (26 Chelonia, 20 Crocodylia, 31 Sauria and 24 Serpentes) in danger of extinction. International conferences (Washington Convention, 1973, Berne Convention, 1979, and Bonn Convention, 1979) have passed resolutions designed to prohibit or at least to reduce the trading and capture of specimens belonging to rare species; and some countries have introduced laws for the protection of reptiles and of the natural habitats frequented by the most endangered species. Strict measures of protection have helped to ensure the survival of the New Zealand tuatara (*Sphenodon punctatus*) and the giant Galápagos tortoise (*Geochelone elephantopus*); but it must be admitted that in the majority of instances protective measures adopted by international conventions and by individual nations have not been very effective, either because they do not go far enough or because they are difficult to apply.

For all these reasons the future of reptiles looks more and more uncertain, and it may not be long before the crocodiles and marine turtles vanish forever from our rivers and seas. Although many people are unlikely to be greatly saddened by this prospect, our own future is affected and we should in fact be extremely concerned about such an event. Archie Carr wrote in 1969 that reptiles inhabited the earth when nature was still wild and these were the surroundings which saw the development of the nervous and endocrine systems that, from our distant ancestor, led to the appearance of humans. If we allow the reptiles to disappear, it is a sign that everything wild will disappear. And if that happens we ourselves will no longer be truly human.

Herpetological organizations and journals. In order to stimulate interest and coordinate and promote professional and non-professional activities in herpetology, associations devoted specifically to amphibians and reptiles have been founded in many countries. A lengthy list of herpetological societies and journals throughout the world was published in *Herpetological Circular* No. 13 (1983) issued by the Society for the Study of Amphibians and Reptiles, and anyone seeking more information on the subject will find it useful to consult this publication. The following list therefore merely lists the names of major organizations and journals:

The Herpetological Association of Africa, Bloemfontein, South Africa (publishes the *Journal of the Herpetological Association of Africa*)
American Society of Ichthyologists and Herpetologists, Gainesville, Florida, USA (publishes the journal *Copeia*).
Australasian Affiliation of Herpetological Societies, Sydney, Australia (publishes the journal *Herpetofauna*).
The British Herpetological Society, London, United Kingdom (publishes *The British Journal of Herpetology*, now known as *The Herpetological Journal*).

(Continued on page 125)

The table below shows the geographical distribution of the families belonging to the four orders of living reptiles.

Table 2

Order CHELONIA
Fam. Carettochelyidae
Southern New Guinea and northern Australia
Fam. Chelydridae
North and Central America, northwestern South America
Fam. Cheloniidae
Warm and temperate seas throughout the world
Fam. Dermatemydidae
Central America
Fam. Dermochelyidae
Warm and temperate seas throughout the world
Fam. Emydidae
North, Central, and South America, West Indies, Europe, northwest Africa, Asia Minor, southern and eastern Asia
Fam. Kinosternidae
North, Central, and South America
Fam. Staurotypidae
Central America
Fam. Testudinidae
Southern North America, South America, Galápagos Islands, southern Europe, Africa, Madagascar, Aldabra Atoll, Asia Minor, central and southern Asia
Fam. Trionychidae
North America, Africa, Asia Minor, southern and eastern Asia, New Guinea
Fam. Platysternidae
Southeast Asia

Order PLEURODIRA
Fam. Chelidae
South America, Australia, New Guinea
Fam. Pelomedusidae
South America, central-southern Africa, Madagascar, Seychelles, Mauritius

Order SQUAMATA
Suborder Sauria
Fam. Agamidae
Southeast Europe, Africa, Asia Minor, central, southern and eastern Asia, New Guinea, Australia
Fam. Chamaeleontidae
Southern Spain, Africa, Madagascar, Asia Minor, southwest Arabia, India, Sri Lanka
Fam. Iguanidae
North, Central, and South America, West Indies, Galápagos Islands, Madagascar, Fiji, Tonga

Fam. Gekkonidae
> Southern United States, Central and South America, West Indies, southern Europe, Africa, Madagascar, Asia Minor, central, southern and eastern Asia, New Guinea, Australia, New Zealand

Fam. Pygopodidae
> New Guinea and Australia

Fam. Teiidae
> North, Central and South America, West Indies

Fam. Lacertidae
> Europe, Africa, Asia, Indo-Australian Archipelago

Fam. Xantusiidae
> Central America, Cuba, southwestern North America

Fam. Scincidae
> North, Central and South America, West Indies, southern Europe, Africa, Madagascar, Seychelles, Asia Minor, central, southern and eastern Asia, New Guinea, Australia, New Zealand, Polynesia, Micronesia

Fam. Cordylidae
> Central and southern Africa, Madagascar

Fam. Dibamidae
> Eastern Mexico, Indochina, Indonesia, New Guinea, Philippines

Fam. Xenosauridae
> Central America, southern Cuba

Fam. Anguidae
> North, Central and South America, West Indies, Europe, northwest Africa, Asia Minor, southern Asia

Fam. Helodermatidae
> Southwestern United States, Mexico, Guatemala

Fam. Lanthanotidae
> Borneo

Fam. Varanidae
> Africa, Asia Minor, Arabia, southern Asia, New Guinea, Australia

Order SQUAMATA
Suborder Serpentes
Fam. Leptotyphlopidae
> Southwestern United States, Central and South America, West Indies, Africa, Asia Minor, Arabia, southwest Asia

Fam. Typhlopidae
> Central and South America, West Indies, southeast Europe, central, southern, and eastern Africa, southern Asia, New Guinea, Australia

Fam. Anomalepididae
> Central and South America

Fam. Aniliidae
> Northern South America, Sri Lanka, southeast Asia

Fam. Uropeltidae
India and Sri Lanka
Fam. Xenopeltidae
Southeast Asia
Fam. Boidae
Western North America, Central and South America, West Indies, southeast Europe, Africa, Madagascar, Asia Minor, central and southern Asia, New Guinea, Australia, Fiji, Solomons
Fam. Acrochordidae
Southeast Asia, New Guinea, northern Australia, Solomons
Fam. Colubridae
North, Central and South America, West Indies, Galápagos, Europe, Africa, Madagascar, Asia, New Guinea, northern and eastern Australia
Fam. Elapidae (1)
Southern United States, Central and South America, Africa, Asia Minor, Arabia, southern and eastern Asia, New Guinea, Australia
Fam. Biperidae
North, Central and South America, Europe, Africa, Asia

Order SQUAMATA (Amphisbaenia)
Fam. Amphisbaenidae (2)
Southeastern United States, West Indies, South America, Spain, northwest, central-west and southern Africa, Asia Minor
Fam. Bipedidae
Northwest Mexico
Fam. Trogonophidae
Northwest Africa, Somalia, Arabia, western Iran, Iraq, southern Kuwait
Fam. Rhynchocephalia Sphenodontidae
Small islands off coasts of New Zealand

Order CROCODYLIA
Fam. Alligatoridae
Southeastern United States, Central and South America, eastern China
Fam. Crocodylidae
Southern Florida, West Indies, Central America and northern South America, Africa, Madagascar, southern Asia, Indonesia, New Guinea, northern Australia
Fam. Gabialidae
Pakistan, northern India, Nepal, Bangladesh

(1) The seasnakes, which live in marine zones close to tropical coasts of the Pacific and Indian oceans (absent from the Atlantic), are nowadays often ascribed to this family, though often placed in a family of their own (Hydrophiidae).
(2) The only species of this family belonging to the genus Rhineura (*R. floridana*) is ascribed by some herpetologists to the family Rhineuridae.

(Continued from page 121)

Chinese Society of Herpetologists, Chengdu, China (publishes the journal *Acta Herpetologica Sinica*).

Deutsche Gesellschaft für Herpetologie und Terrarienkunde, Frankfurt-am-Main, Federal Republic of Germany (publishes the journal *Salamandra*).

Herpetologists' League, Lawrence, Kansas, USA (publishes the journal *Herpetologica* and *Herpetological Monographs*).

The Herpetological Society of Japan, Kyoto, Japan (publishes the *Japanese Journal of Herpetology*).

Nederlandse Vereniging voor Herpetologie en Terrariumkunde, Amsterdam, The Netherlands (publishes the journal *Lacerta*).

Societas Europaea Herpetologica, Leiden, The Netherlands (publishes the journal *Amphibia-Reptilia*).

Société Batrachologique de France, Paris, France (publishes the journal *Alytes*).

Société Herpétologique de France, Paris, France (publishes the *Bulletin de la Société Herpétologique de France*).

Society for the Study of Amphibians and Reptiles, Athens, Ohio, USA (publishes the *Journal of Herpetology*, *Herpetological Review*, and various monographs)

81 CHELYDRA SERPENTINA
Snapping turtle

Classification Order Chelonia, Family Chelydridae.
Distribution North, Central and South America, from Canada to Ecuador.
Identification This large turtle has an oval carapace, gray, brown or olive-brown, with three prominent longitudinal ridges and a deeply serrated rear margin. The plastron is relatively small, cross-shaped, yellowish or brown. The head is huge, with small eyes and powerful jaws. The legs are long and sturdy, and the feet are fully webbed. The tail is as long as the carapace and topped with saw-toothed keels. Length of carapace: 8–19 in (20–48 cm).
Habitat Soft-bottomed swamps, ponds, lakes, rivers; also enters brackish waters.
Biology The snapper is a species with strictly aquatic habits. It likes to settle on the bottom of ponds and can stay hidden under the mud, awaiting prey, for quite long periods. It feeds on aquatic invertebrates and plants, carrion, diseased fish, amphibians, and birds. The adults breed from April to November; in late spring, the females travel to sunny nesting sites (often some distance from water) where they lay 25–80 eggs. Hatching occurs in 9–18 weeks.

---

82 CARETTA CARETTA
Loggerhead turtle

Classification Order Chelonia, Family Cheloniidae.
Distribution Atlantic, Western Pacific and Indian oceans, and Mediterranean and Black seas.
Identification The loggerhead has an elongated, heart-shaped carapace, reddish-brown, covered with horny plates and with five pairs of costal scutes. The plastron is yellowish, with two longitudinal ridges in the young. The head appears proportionately huge. The forelegs are bigger than the hind pair, and both are transformed into broad, flat flippers. Length of carapace: 31–48 in (79–122 cm).
Habitat Warm and temperate seas all over the world.
Biology This is an exclusively marine species which frequents estuaries, lagoons, and coastal bays in search of crustaceans, molluscs, and fishes. As a consequence, many are accidently caught in shrimp and fishing nets. Females concentrate in the coastal waters of the area chosen for egg-laying and during the night in high tide periods, climb up the beaches to deposit about 120 spherical eggs in deep holes dug in the sand. The eggs hatch after about 2–3 months of incubation, and sexual maturity is attained at 8–12 years of age.

83 CHELONIA MYDAS
Green turtle

Classification Order Chelonia, Family Cheloniidae.
Distribution Atlantic, Pacific and Indian oceans, Mediterranean and Black seas.
Identification The green turtle has a large, heart-shaped carapace, dark brown or olive, covered with horny plates and with four pairs of costal scutes. They have a single pair of prefrontal scales between their eyes. The horny sheath covering the upper jaw is never curved. The legs are transformed into large, powerful flippers. In young individuals there is a vertebral ridge and, on the plastron, two lateral ridges. Length of carapace: 28–60 in (71–153 cm).
Habitat Warm seas all over the world.
Biology This turtle usually lives in areas of sea close to coasts where it feeds on turtle grass and other marine plants. The reptile is widely hunted, however, for calipee, a substance used for making an appetizing soup. The species is everywhere endangered; according to the data of the IUCN, there are very few areas throughout the tropics where the green turtle can breed undisturbed. Green turtles, as other marine turtles, return to the beaches where they were born to nest. Females nest every 2 to 4 years, 2–8 times a season they deposit about 100 spherical eggs.

---

84 DERMOCHELYS CORIACEA
Leatherback turtle

Classification Order Chelonia, Family Dermochelyidae.
Distribution Atlantic, Pacific and Indian oceans, Mediterranean sea.
Identification This is the largest living turtle and is distinguished from all others by the particular structure of its carapace, which has no horny plates and is formed of small bony plaques, joined together in a mosaic pattern, and embedded in the extremely strong, leathery skin. There are seven prominent keels on the carapace. The plastron is white and bears 5 ridges. The head is large and round, with powerful jaws. The legs are transformed into heavy flippers which lack claws. Length of carapace: 48–84 in (122–213 cm).
Habitat Chiefly tropical and subtropical seas but deep into temperate waters in summer.
Biology The leatherback is a critically endangered species. Although they are generally not eaten, their eggs are prized. Many leatherbacks die annually after ingesting plastic bags and other floating trash which they confuse for jellyfish, their main diet. Others perish in fishing nets and from injuries suffered from encounters with boats. These powerful swimmers travel great distances at sea. They home to natal beaches to breed and lay their eggs.

85 CHRYSEMYS PICTA
Painted turtle

Classification Order Chelonia, Family Emydidae.
Distribution Southern Canada and United States.
Identification This species has a smooth, flattened, black or olive, oval carapace, with bright red bars on marginal scutes. The head and neck are olive-green with very conspicuous yellow or red stripes. There are narrow red bands, too, on the legs, and the feet have strong claws. The plastron is completely yellow in eastern and southern parts of the range, and yellow with dark markings among those from central and western regions. Length of carapace: 4–9⅞ in (10–25 cm). (9⅞ in = record length.)
Habitat Ponds, lakes, slow-running rivers.
Biology The painted turtle is particularly common in muddy ponds or lake coves with plenty of vegetation. The young are carnivorous, feeding on aquatic insects, crustaceans, and tadpoles, while the adults are almost wholly vegetarian. The eggs hatch after 2–3 months' incubation. Females in northern populations nest once or twice a year, those in the south 2–4. Clutch size ranges from 2–20 eggs.

---

86 TRACHEMYS SCRIPTA
Pond slider

Classification Order Chelonia, Family Emydidae.
Distribution Widespread in central and southeastern United States and Mexico, south through Central America to northern Colombia and Venezuela; introduced in Africa and southern Asia.
Identification This species has a weakly keeled, oval carapace which is dark brown or greenish with transverse yellow bars, reticulations, or eye-like spots. The neck bears a prominent yellow, orange, or red blotch or stripe behind the eye. The red-eared slider, *c. s. elegans* (illustrated here), from the Mississippi Valley has a long bright reddish stripe on its tympanum. The plastron is yellowish, plain to intricately patterned. Length of carapace: 5–11⅜ in (13–29 cm).
Habitat Swamps, ponds, lakes and slow-moving rivers.
Biology The pond slider is active by day and frequents waters with muddy bottoms, plenty of plant growth, and basking logs. The young feed on snails, tadpoles, insects, and crustaceans, while the adults are chiefly vegetarian. In the United States, mating occurs from March to June. One to three clutches of eggs are laid in early summer in earthen nests; they hatch after 2 months' incubation.

87 EMYS ORBICULARIS
European pond turtle

Classification Order Chelonia, Family Emydidae.
Distribution Northwestern Africa, Europe (except northern areas), and western Asia.
Identification The species has a flat, oval carapace, dark brown or blackish, with numerous yellowish spots or streaks. The plastron is dark brown or brown with yellow markings. Yellow spots or vermiculations are present on the head, neck, and limbs; they sometimes fuse to form irregular bands. The adult male generally has a slightly concave plastron. Length of carapace: 5–7½ in (13–19 cm).
Habitat Ponds, swamps, canals, lakes.
Biology This terrapin inhabits stagnant or slow-flowing water, and is commonly found in ponds with abundant vegetation and with little risk of human disturbance. It is active mainly by day and spends long periods on sunny banks, ready to dive into the water at the slightest alarm. It feeds on invertebrates, small fish and amphibians, hunting its prey both in water and on land. Females lay about 4 to 10 eggs in holes dug in the sandy banks. The young, barely 1 in (2 cm) long hatch after 2–3 months' incubation.

88 MALAYEMYS SUBTRIJUGA
Malayan snail-eating turtle

Classification Order Chelonia, Family Emydidae.
Distribution Thailand to southern Vietnam south through Malaysia to Sumatra and Java.
Identification This turtle has a dark brown carapace, with three distinct longitudinal ridges. The scutes of the plastron, which is almost uniformly brown or blackish, have a narrow yellowish border. The head is fairly large and flat, with a prominent yellow or whitish stripe extending from the nostril over the eye to the neck. A narrower stripe runs from the tip of the snout along the upper jaw onto the neck. Length of carapace: 8–14 in (20–35 cm).
Habitat Marshes, canals, rivers.
Biology The Malayan snail-eating turtle frequents stagnant or slow-flowing water in lowland areas. During the day it rests on banks or on floating mats of plants, but it is extremely vigilant and at the least alarm dives into the water, vanishing among the vegetation on the bottom. It feeds mainly on molluscs, grinding them with its powerful jaws, but occasionally preys on crustaceans and insect larvae as well. Females lay their eggs in holes dug in the sandy banks.

89 MAUREMYS CASPICA
Caspian pond turtle

Classification   Order Chelonia, Family Emydidae.
Distribution   Southeastern Europe and southwestern Asia.
Identification   The flattened carapace is olive-green or grayish-brown, with a prominent vertebral keel. The plastron is yellow, with variously shaped and patterned black markings. The head is dark green, with yellow stripes bordered in black, which extend onto the neck. In the young, the costal scutes and those at the edges of the carapace are adorned with bright yellowish or reddish markings. Length of carapace: 4–9 in (10–23 cm).
Habitat   Ponds, swamps, lakes, rivers and slow-flowing streams.
Biology   The Caspian pond turtle is predominantly aquatic and is usually found in shallow ponds and lakes with plenty of plant growth. It strays only a short distance, and for brief periods, from the water and normally spends much of the day basking on banks in the sun, ready to dive in at the slightest sign of danger. It is a carnivore, feeding chiefly on molluscs, amphibians and small fish. Like other Emydidae, the eggs are laid in nests dug in the sand and hatch after 3 months' incubation.

---

90 TERRAPENE CAROLINA
Eastern box turtle

Classification   Order Chelonia, Family Emydidae.
Distribution   Eastern United States, from Maine and Michigan southward to eastern Texas and south Florida.
Identification   The strange common name of this species is derived from the structure of the shell, which is made up of a high domed carapace, similar to that of a tortoise, and a large plastron, provided with a transverse hinge located between the pectoral and abdominal scutes. Thanks to this hinge, the anterior and posterior lobes of the plastron are movable, thus permitting close contact with the anterior and posterior margins of the carapace. When the animal is frightened, it withdraws its head, legs and tail into the shell and moves the two lobes of the plastron, enclosing itself inside an impregnable box of horny plates. Length of carapace: 4–8½ in (10–22 cm).
Habitat   Moist woodlands, wet meadows, and floodplains.
Biology   The Eastern box turtle is predominantly terrestrial. It is usually seen after rain or early in the day. Its diet is extremely varied, comprising earthworms, slugs, insects, and wild berries. In summer it moves to the margins of swamps or marshlands. Females lay their eggs in May–July, and these usually hatch in late summer.

91 KINOSTERNON SUBRUBRUM
Mud turtle

Classification Order Chelonia, Family Kinosternidae.
Distribution Eastern United States, from Long Island to eastern Texas and north in the Mississippi Valley to Indiana.
Identification The carapace is moderately dome-shaped, smooth, oval, brown or olive, and patternless. The head is usually dark brown, with lighter spots and streaks. The yellow to brown plastron is double-hinged and has 11 scutes. Its transverse hinges of connective tissue are mobile and can completely close the front and rear openings of the shell when the head, legs and tail are retracted. Length of carapace: 3–4⅞ in (8–12 cm).
Habitat Swampy parts of rivers, slow-running streams, brackish lagoons.
Biology The mud turtle is a semi-aquatic species. It prefers bodies of fresh water with plenty of vegetation but is also found in brackish pools. It hunts invertebrates, caught as a rule in the muddy depths. Adults mate in spring, and in June the females lay 1–6 elliptical eggs in holes dug in sandy soil or among plant detritus.

---

92 STERNOTHERUS ODORATUS
Stinkpot turtle

Classification Order Chelonia, Family Kinosternidae.
Distribution Southeastern Canada and eastern United States.
Identification The carapace is highly domed and moderately long, dark gray or olive-brown and may be smooth or have 3 keels. The plastron is very small and has a single inconspicuous hinge of connective tissue which links the anterior lobe to the central part of the plastron itself. Two light stripes extend from nostril to neck, passing respectively above and beneath the eye. The tail is broad and short, terminating in a blunt horny nail in the male and a sharp horny tip (sometimes absent) in the female. Length of carapace: 3–5⅜ in (8–14 cm).
Habitat Swamps, ponds, lakes, canals.
Biology The stinkpot turtle is strictly aquatic and mainly inhabits muddy-bottomed waters with plenty of plant growth. It may leave the water to bask in the sun on a tree trunk or on masses of floating plants, but is always ready to dive in at the least sign of danger. When disturbed, it emits a foul-smelling yellow secretion from its musk glands under the margin of its carapace. The females lay their eggs from February to June, and they hatch after 2–3 months' incubation. Stinkpots bite and are difficult to handle safely.

93 GEOCHELONE ELEPHANTOPUS
Galapagos tortoise

Classification   Order Chelonia, Family Testudinidae.
Distribution   Galapagos Islands (Ecuador).
Identification   This gigantic tortoise typically has a highly domed carapace, a very big plastron, and a rather small head supported by a long neck. The massive, columnar rear legs and elephantine forelegs are protected by bony-cored scales. Individuals from different populations exhibit different shell shapes. Some are classically dome-shaped, others "saddle-backed," or intermediate. Specimens on some islands rarely reach 150 lb (70 kg), while individuals on other islands may weigh up to 500 lb (227 kg). Length of carapace: 32–48 in (80–122 cm).
Habitat   Dry land, with plenty of succulent plants at least on some islands.
Biology   The Galapagos tortoises mainly occupy the driest and flattest parts of the islands, but often venture up to the volcanic highlands where there is plenty of water and vegetation, using paths trodden from time immemorial. In these surroundings they bathe for long periods in pools and feed on the fruit and flowers of various plants. The adults mate at virtually any time of year. Each female lays about 4–10 large spherical eggs in a hole dug in the ground.

94 GOPHERUS AGASSIZII
Desert tortoise

Classification   Order Chelonia, Family Testudinidae.
Distribution   Extreme southwestern United States and northwestern Mexico.
Identification   This tortoise has an oblong, fairly domed brown carapace, heavily armored front legs for digging, and stumpy elephantine hind legs. The plastron is yellowish with brown along scute margins, and bears a prominent projection on the anterior lobe. The male's plastron is concave. The head is small and reddish-brown. The tail is very short. Length of carapace: 9–14½ in (23–37 cm). (The accompanying photograph shows an albino specimen.)
Habitat   Dry, sandy or gravelly ground, with thorny vegetation and cacti.
Biology   The desert tortoise is active almost exclusively in the early hours of the morning and at dusk, spending most of the day and extremely hot periods inside specially dug underground burrows. During brief sorties in the open, it seeks food, mostly succulent plants. The adults mate in early spring, and in May the females lay 2–14 eggs in funnel-shaped 6 in (15 cm) chambers dug at burrow mouths. The eggs hatch in late summer.

95 GEOCHELONE GIGANTEA
Aldabra turtle

Classification   Order Chelonia, Family Testudinidae.
Distribution   Aldabra, Seychelles Islands; introduced on Mauritius and Reunion islands.
Identification   This large tortoise resembles, in size and looks, the dome-shelled types of Galapagos tortoise, and like the latter is a fairly uniform dark brown or grayish in color. The carapace is noticeably domed, formed of horny plates with numerous concentric grooves. The nuchal scute, absent in the Galapagos species, is almost always evident. The head is small, the neck long and quite strong. The legs, enormous and covered with horny scales, are equipped with large, powerful claws. The tail is extremely short, with a horny claw-like spur at the tip. Length of carapace: 32–48 in (81–122 cm). Giant specimens may exceed 500 lb (227 kg).
Habitat   Scrublands near water holes.
Biology   The species belongs to a group of giant tortoises that once inhabited islands of the Indian Ocean, including the Comoros and Madagascar, which have long since been wiped out by man. Today it roams wild only on the atoll of Aldabra, which consists of four main islands. There are estimated to be some 150,000 individuals living there.

96 TESTUDO GRAECA
Spur-thighed tortoise

Classification   Order Chelonia, Family Testudinidae.
Distribution   Northern Africa, southwestern Europe, southwestern Asia.
Identification   This tortoise has an oval carapace, yellowish or olive-brown with various black spots, with a single super-caudal scute at the back of the carapace above the tail. The plastron is fairly big and, in the male, obviously concave. The legs are quite robust; spurs are present on the thighs. The head is small and the tail extremely short and lacks a large scale on its tip. Length of carapace: 4–11 in (10–27 cm).
Habitat   Scrubland, pine forests and woods of evergreen oaks in coastal areas, sand dunes.
Biology   The spur-thighed tortoise lives in a variety of habitats and is commonly found in fields with bushes on a gentle slope. It is active from March to October and spends the winter latent period inside burrows dug in the ground. It feeds mainly on grass, roots and fruit, but its diet is often complemented by earthworms and snails. Mating, preceded by fierce fights among the courting males, occurs in the spring, while egg-laying takes place in early summer.

97 TESTUDO HERMANNI
Hermann's tortoise

Classification Order Chelonia, Family Testudinidae.
Distribution Southern Europe: southern France to Romania and European Turkey.
Identification This species is very similar in appearance and dimensions to the spur-thighed tortoise. It differs from the latter, however, in having a horny spur at the tip of the tail, a carapace with a divided supercaudal scute above the tail, and no spurs on the thighs. The carapace is yellow with numerous blackish spots. The plastron is also yellow with a number of black marks on the sides, sometimes flowing together to form two broad longitudinal bands. Length of carapace: 4–10½ in (10–27 cm).
Habitat Grassy and shrubby areas, sparse woodlands in coastal areas, sand dunes.
Biology Hermann's tortoise is particularly attracted to scrub-covered rocky hillsides. It is active mainly in the morning and late afternoon, normally spending the hottest part of the day in the shade of bushes. It has a fairly varied diet, feeding on plants and small invertebrates. In the breeding season the males become extremely aggressive and court the females passionately. Eggs are laid in summer and hatch after 3–4 months' incubation.

---

98 TRIONYX SINENSIS
Chinese softshell

Classification Order Chelonia, Family Trionychidae.
Distribution Eastern China, Korea, northern Vietnam, Japan. Introduced into Hawaii.
Identification The species has a carapace and plastron without horny scutes and covered with fairly tough skin. The snout is trunklike and the nostrils are at the tip. The limbs are fairly flattened, and both the hind feet and the fore feet are webbed, only the three inner toes being provided with claws. The upper part of the shell has many small tubercles, arranged in long rows, and is olive-green, with a few black spots. The plastron is very small, yellowish with large dark markings. Length of carapace: 4–10 in (10–25 cm).
Habitat Rivers, lakes, canals, slow-flowing streams.
Biology The Chinese softshell is strictly aquatic, found particularly in lakes and rivers of the Far East. It swims with great agility and feeds on fish, crustaceans and molluscs, caught during the night at the bottom of ponds. The adults are territorial and breed in spring. The eggs, laid in holes dug on the river and lake banks, need 2–3 months' incubation.

99 TRIONYX SPINIFERUS
Spiny softshell

Classification Order Chelonia, Family Trionychidae.
Distribution Southeastern Canada, and central and eastern United States into northeastern Mexico.
Identification Like the Chinese softshell, this species has a pancake-like shell devoid of horny scutes. The carapace has spiny tubercles on its leading edge and is olive or brown with black-bordered eyespots or with dark blotches and a thin dark line around the shell's margin. The plastron is very small, whitish or yellowish. On either side of the head, are two dark-bordered stripes. The limbs are flattened and the toes are joined by broad webs. Length of carapace: males 5–9 in (13–23 cm), females 7–18 in (18–46 cm).
Habitat Lakes, ponds, rivers, streams, marshes.
Biology The Eastern spiny softshell is found in a number of aquatic environments, particularly in rivers and ponds with low, sandy banks. By day it basks in the sun on banks or floating logs; during the night it hunts for food, principally fish, amphibians and crustaceans. The females lay their eggs on the banks of ponds and rivers, from May to August. They hatch at the end of summer or in early autumn.

---

100 CHELODINA LONGICOLLIS
Australian snake-necked turtle

Classification Order Chelonia, Family Chelidae.
Distribution Southeastern Australia.
Identification The turtle has an extremely long neck, cylindrical in shape, covered with warty skin. This curious neck cannot be retracted into the shell and, when the animal is frightened, is folded sideways under the rim of the carapace. The upper part of the shell, smooth and fairly flat, is rich brown to black. The plastron is white or cream, with black-bordered sutures between the scutes. The head is relatively flat and uniformly grayish. The front and rear feet have broad inter-digital webs and four sharp claws. Length of carapace: 4–10 in (10–25 cm).
Habitat Marshes, ponds, swampy areas of river, oxbow lakes.
Biology The long-necked turtle is strictly aquatic and occupies a large number of habitats. It often basks on semi-submerged rocks or masses of floating vegetation, but is always vigilant and at the slightest hint of danger plunges into the water, where it swims with great agility. It feeds on small fish, tadpoles, crustaceans and mollusks, catching its prey by striking out with its snake-like neck. If molested it can emit a foul-smelling whitish glandular secretion.

101 PELOMEDUSA SUBRUFA
Helmeted turtle

Classification   Order Chelonia, Family Pelomedusidae.
Distribution   Africa south of Sahara, Madagascar.
Identification   This side-necked turtle has a fairly flat carapace which lacks a plastral hinge. The head is large with two small tentacles under the chin. When the turtle is frightened, it pulls its head to one side under the carapace. Feet are webbed. The carapace is olive to dark brown and the plastron is entirely black, yellowish, or pale-colored with dark lines in the sutures or with a light-centered pattern. The head is dark on top, and pale below. Length of carapace: 8–12½ in (20–32 cm).
Habitat   Slow-moving and quiet waters of many descriptions.
Biology   One of the most common and widely distributed freshwater turtles in Africa, it is especially fond of temporary pools. The turtles are often seen moving about after good rains. Their diet includes aquatic plants, crustaceans, insects, and amphibians. In some areas they are known to ambush small birds drinking at the water's edge. During drought periods, they burrow into the drying bottom to estivate. Females lay 10 to 40 soft-shelled eggs in a flask-shaped pit. The young hatch in three months and emerge after the ground has been softened by rain. Helmeted turtles are belligerent, bite, and have a musky smell.

102 AGAMA AGAMA
Rainbow lizard

Classification   Order Squamata, Family Agamidae.
Distribution   Central Africa.
Identification   The head is triangular, the body solid and flat, the legs well developed and the tail long and powerful. The large ear opening is surrounded by spiny scales. In males, the head and middle portion of tail are bright yellow or orange-red, while the upper parts are bluish or dark gray. The females and young are more or less uniformly brown, with some lighter spots on the nape and flanks. Total length: 12–16 in (30–40 cm).
Habitat   Rocky ground, savannas, edges of woods.
Biology   The common agama is a rock-climbing and tree-dwelling species ranging widely over tropical Africa. It occupies a large variety of habits and is even seen quite often near built-up areas. The adults form family groups which may comprise 2–25 individuals. The members of this group have a strictly demarcated hunting ground and are led by a dominant male who is responsible for the defense of the family nucleus and its territory. During the breeding season the receptive females incite the males to mate by making peculiar movements with their body and tail. Each female normally lays 3–8 eggs. Their diet includes myriad arthropods including spiders, wasps, and beetles.

103 AMPHIBOLURUS BARBATUS
Bearded dragon

Classification   Order Squamata, Family Agamidae.
Distribution   Eastern Australia.
Identification   The bearded lizard has a triangular, broad, flat head, with a series of large spiny scales at the corners of the mouth and above the tympanum. Underneath is a huge throat pouch covered with numerous sharp spines. The body is flattened and heavily built. Color varies from gray or fawn, brown, reddish-brown, to nearly black with a longitudinal row of light spots on either side of the body. Total length: 16–24 in (40–60 cm).
Habitat   Coastal wet sclerophyllous forests to dry interior thorny scrublands.
Biology   This semi-arboreal lizard is typically seen basking on stumps, fence posts, or roadways. When they have reached an optimal body temperature, they hunt for insects, flowers and soft plants. It avoids the heat of the day in deep burrows. If attacked, the bearded dragon assumes a characteristic threat posture, inflating its body, opening its mouth and hugely dilating its big, spiny throat pouch.

104 CALOTES VERSICOLOR
Indian bloodsucker

Classification   Order Squamata, Family Agamidae.
Distribution   Southwestern, southern, and southeastern Asia.
Identification   This species has a relatively small, highly held head and a laterally compressed body, with a small crest formed of thin, pointed horny scales along the vertebral line. The tail is much longer than the body and terminates in an extremely slender tip. The forelimbs are shorter than the hind feet. The coloration of the upper parts may change rapidly when basking or with the state of stress of the animal, ranging from bright green to light brown. In excited males, the head and shoulders become bright red. The males have an inflatable throat pouch and during the mating season their head turns brilliant red. Total length: 12–19½ in (30–49 cm).
Habitat   Tropical rain forests.
Biology   This tree-dwelling reptile is very common in the woodlands of southern Asia where it feeds on insects, spiders, and occasionally nesting birds. In the breeding season the males court the females by distending the throat pouch and rhythmically opening and closing the mouth as he solemnly nods his head up and down. The females lay their eggs in an earthen nest chamber, each clutch consisting of 4–23 eggs.

105 UROMASTYX ACANTHINURUS
Dabb spiny-tailed lizard

Classification Order Squamata, Family Agamidae.
Distribution North Africa and Sinai peninsula.
Identification This lizard has a triangular head and a solid, rather flat body. The club-like tail is broad and short, the top and sides covered with numerous large spiny scales, arranged in transverse rings. The coloration is extremely variable, ranging from yellow or reddish with many reticulations or scribbly markings to grayish with dark transverse stripes, or even uniformly black. Total length: 8–16 in (20–40 cm).
Habitat Rocky desert lands.
Biology The "mastigure" lives in arid, sparsely vegetated areas of the Sahara and is active only in the morning and late afternoon, spending the hottest part of the day in rock clefts or in long, deep burrows dug in the ground. On occasion it eats large insects, but it feeds almost exclusively on leaves and stems of hard shrubs. When pursued by a predator it scuttles rapidly into its burrow, letting the spiny part of its strong tail hang out. If the aggressor continues its attack, the reptile swishes its tail violently from side to side, and this is usually sufficient to discourage even its most deadly enemies. Spiny-tailed lizards are egg layers. Like most reptiles, the number laid varies with size.

106 ANGUIS FRAGILIS
Slow worm

Classification Order Squamata, Family Anguidae.
Distribution Europe (excluding Ireland and many Mediterranean islands) and western Asia.
Identification This saurian has a fairly small head, tiny eyes with mobile lids, and a limbless serpentine body with smooth, highly polished scales. The color varies with age and sex. New born slow worms are yellowish, bronze, golden brown or silvery-green with a vertebral stripe. Adult females are brown, brick-red or copper and may retain the stripe which is faded or lost in the more somber colored males. Blue-spotted males are sometimes found. Females are usually larger than males. Total length: 11–21 in (28–54 cm).
Habitat Woodland edges, grassy meadows, thickets, and heathlands.
Biology The slow worm is found in decaying woodland leaf litter as well as humid situations associated with human activity: rubbish dumps, quarries, gardens, and abandoned farms. It spends the night and the middle of the day beneath stones or fallen trunks, and is a voracious feeder on earthworms, small snails, insects and especially, slugs. Males are normally mild tempered but in the breeding season they become aggressive and may seize one another with their jaws. The females are ovoviviparous and after 3 months' gestation give birth to 3–26 young.

107 GERRHONOTUS MULTICARINATUS
Southern alligator lizard

Classification   Order Squamata, Family Anguidae.
Distribution   Northwestern Mexico and extreme western regions of United States.
Identification   This species has a flat, wedge-shaped head, eyes with a yellow iris and a relatively long body supported by four fairly slender 5-toed limbs. There is a distinct groove on the sides. The tail is longer than the rest of the body and terminates in a thin tip. The back is yellowish or reddish-brown, with a number of dark crossbands. Total length: 10–16½ in (25–42 cm). (16⅞ in = record size.)
Habitat   Oak woodlands, grasslands, chaparral, and damp canyon bottoms in arid lands.
Biology   The alligator lizard is an agile climber and may climb shrubs and trees in search of insects and nestling birds. It also feeds on scorpions, spiders, and slugs which it catches among leaf litter or fresh heaps. When attacked or molested, it reacts by biting its aggressor and violently ejecting feces. The females are oviparous, laying two to three clutches of 1–41 eggs during the warm months.

108 OPHISAURUS APODUS
Scheltopusik

Classification   Order Squamata, Family Anguidae.
Distribution   Southeastern Europe, and parts of south-western and central Asia.
Identification   This species has a snake-like body with large glossy ridged scales with bony plates, a large head, and eyes with round pupils and closable eye-lids. The body is quite long and has a prominent groove on either side. There are no forelegs and the back legs are reduced to two tiny cylindrical stumps on either side of the cloacal opening. Adults are usually uniformly brown while young animals are gray with dark transverse bars. Total length: 32–55 in (81–140 cm).
Habitat   Woodland clearings and fringes, rocky hillsides.
Biology   The habits of "glass snake" or glass lizard are similar to those of the slow worm. It prefers fairly dry areas and frequents stone walls and rocky areas. It is active in the morning and late afternoon and after rain storms. Its diet is extremely varied but it feeds mainly on snails, insects and small mammals. As a rule it wriggles slowly over the ground but when molested will slither off rapidly with serpentine movements. The females are oviparous and lay 6–12 elongated eggs. These hatch after 2 months' incubation. They are long-lived. Some captives have lived more than 20 years.

109 OPHISAURUS VENTRALIS
Eastern glass lizard

Classification   Order Squamata, Family Anguidae.
Distribution   Coastal plains of southeastern United States from North Carolina to Louisiana.
Identification   This saurian has a small head which is hardly distinguishable from the body, with closable eye-lids. The limbs are entirely absent and there is a distinct longitudinal groove on the flanks. The upper parts of the adults are greenish, with numerous longitudinal black lines or dashes extending from head to tail, but the young are khaki colored with a broad, dark longitudinal stripe on either side of the body. Total length: 18–42⅝ in (46–108 cm).
Habitat   Wet grasslands, coastal pine flatwoods, tropical hardwood hammocks.
Biology   This glass lizard is usually seen during the early morning hours in damp grassy areas where it forages for snails, insects, spiders, other lizards and small snakes. It is a good burrower and spends much of its life in an underground retreat. Females lay 8–17 eggs and coil about them to protect them during their two-month incubation.

---

110 CHAMAELEO BITAENIATUS
Double-banded chameleon

Classification   Order Squamata, Family Chamaeleontidae.
Distribution   East Africa.
Identification   The body is somewhat compressed laterally, the head narrow with a high bony helmet and distinct throat crest. The vertebral line is marked by a low crest of dark, conical tubercles extending from the rear of the head to the tail. The color of the back is somewhat variable and may be brownish, dark brown or blackish. There are almost always two light longitudinal bands on the flanks. Total length: 4–7¾ in (10–20 cm).
Habitat   Savannas, wooded hillsides, and mountain forests.
Biology   Strictly arboreal, this master of color change spends the early part of the morning warming up in the sun; only when it has reached an optimum body temperature does it slowly move to an ambush station where it will wait for hours for their prey to pass. It feeds predominantly on insects, and, like all other chameleons, catches them by "shooting" victims with its extremely long, sticky tongue. The adults are markedly territorial and normally occupy the same tree for a considerable time. The females are ovoviviparous and give birth to 10–25 young.

111 CHAMAELEO CHAMELEON
Mediterranean chameleon

Classification Order Squamata, Family Chamaeleontidae.
Distribution North Africa, southern Iberian peninsula, Crete, southwestern Asia.
Identification The body is laterally compressed, the head narrow and high, the eyes fairly big and protected by fused lids with a small opening for the pupil. The eyes move independently of one another. In adults the back of the head bears a bony helmet in the shape of a triangular pyramid. As in other chameleons, the feet are modified into grasping pincers, with the toes divided into groups of two outer and three inner toes on the front limbs and the reverse arrangement on the hind limbs. The tail is prehensile. The chameleon's color changes according to the animal's emotional state and health, and may be gray, green or brown, with or without spots and longitudinal stripes on the flanks. Total length: 8–12 in (20–30 cm).
Habitat Scrub, thickets, and bushy grasslands.
Biology Unlike most chameleons which are strongly arboreal, this species sometimes descends to the ground where it moves around slowly and awkwardly. It is active only by day and feeds principally on insects. Adults are solitary and territorial and extremely aggressive toward intruders. The females are oviparous and lay their eggs in cavities dug at the foot of bushes.

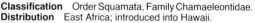

112 CHAMAELEO JACKSONI
Jackson's chameleon

Classification Order Squamata, Family Chamaeleontidae.
Distribution East Africa; introduced into Hawaii.
Identification Males have three long, pointed, front-facing horns, two above the eyes, the third, slightly longer, at the tip of the snout. Horns are absent or weakly developed in the female. At the back of the head is a small crested helmet. Along the vertebral line is a crest of spiny tubercles, fairly widely separated. As in other chameleons, the body coloration is very variable, green, brown or brownish-yellow, with or without spots. Total length: 6–13¾ in (15–35 cm).
Habitat Mountain thickets and forests.
Biology This "three-horned" chameleon is a resident of the East African highlands and lives exclusively in trees and shrubs. It is active mainly in the morning and late afternoon, feeding on various insects. Males are markedly territorial and during the breeding season behave aggressively toward rivals, attacking with their horns. The females are ovoviviparous, giving birth to 7–40 young at a time.

113 CORDYLUS GIGANTEUS
Sungazer

Classification Order Squamata, Family Cordylidae.
Distribution Southern Africa.
Identification This lizard has a triangular, flattened head and a stout body with large spiny scales, slanting backward and upward, on the head, flanks, hind legs and powerful tail. The upper part of the head is dark brown, the lower yellow. Body and tail are more or less yellow with some touches of brown. Total length: 8–15¾ in (20–40 cm).
Habitat Dry, rocky ground and grasslands.
Biology This giant girdled lizard is broadly known as the sungazer because, when it exposes its body to the sun's warming rays in the morning, it stays almost motionless for quite some time, supported on its forelegs, head pointing skywards. When it has reached optimum temperature it becomes extremely active and goes hunting for spiders, termites, grasshoppers and beetles. They live in colonies in a cluster of 5-ft (1.5-m) long burrows. Although females may share their retreat with juveniles, each burrow is usually occupied by a single animal. If pursued into its tunnel by a predator, it will lash its armored tail back and forth and bury the spines on its head into the tunnel roof. One or two young are born in February or March.

---

114 HELODERMA SUSPECTUM
Gila monster

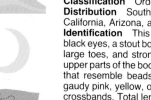

Classification Order Squamata, Family Helodermatidae.
Distribution Southwestern United States (Utah, Nevada, California, Arizona, and New Mexico) and northern Mexico.
Identification This lizard has a large, broad head, small black eyes, a stout body supported by short legs with big feet, large toes, and strong claws, and a short swollen tail. The upper parts of the body and the limbs are covered with scales that resemble beads. The snout is black and followed by gaudy pink, yellow, or orange and black reticulations and/or crossbands. Total length: 16–22 in (41–56 cm).
Habitat Desert scrub and arid grasslands into dry juniper-oak woodlands.
Biology This species and the Mexican beaded lizard (*Heloderma horridum*) are the only living venomous lizards. The venom, used principally to immobilize prey, is extremely dangerous for humans as well. The gila monster is diurnally active and its peak surface activity is the springtime. These carnivores specialize on the young of nesting rodents, rabbits, and birds. The eggs of reptiles and ground-nesting birds are also taken. More than 95 percent of the gila monster's life is spent underground which has long given the impression that they were rare and nocturnal. Nesting females deposit 2–12 eggs in summer, take 10 months to develop, and hatch the following spring.

115 COLEONYX VARIEGATUS
Banded gecko

Classification Order Squamata, Family Gekkonidae.
Distribution Southwestern United States (Nevada, California, Utah and Arizona) and northern Mexico.
Identification The head is large and raised at the back. The eyes, with vertical pupils, are protected by movable eyelids. The skin of the upper part of the body is extremely flexible and delicate and is covered by small granules. The limbs and toes are slender. The back and the tail are pinkish or yellowish with broad transverse brown or blackish stripes. Total length: 4½–6 in (11–15 cm).
Habitat Desert scrub, dry juniper-oak woodlands, arid grasslands, and chaparral.
Biology This velvet-skinned lizard is typically found in rocky situations but also can be encountered in barren desert dunes. It is exclusively nocturnal, spending the day hidden in rock fissures or inside rodents' burrows. It is quite agile and speedy, and feeds on various insects and spiders. When attacked by a predator it does not stand its ground but flees rapidly, often leaving behind its tail which readily breaks at the basal constriction if grabbed. During the breeding season, males, before mating, confront one another in ritual duels. The females lay two or more clutches, usually of two eggs, in spring and summer. They hatch in 6–8 weeks.

---

116 GEKKO GECKO
Tokay gecko

Classification Order Squamata, Family Gekkonidae.
Distribution India, Burma, southern China, Indochina, Malaccan peninsula, Indonesia, Philippines.
Identification This gekko has a large, flat head and big eyes with a vertical pupil and yellow iris. The upper body is covered with small juxtaposed granules and large hemispherical tubercles. The digits of the hands and feet are narrow at the base and enlarged at the tip, with a series of adhesive pads on the lower surface. The color of the body is blue-gray to brownish-gray, with numerous deep blue and reddish-orange spots on the back. Total length: 11–14 in (28–35 cm).
Habitat Tree trunks of tropical forests, ruins, walls of old buildings.
Biology Although the species frequents many natural habitats, it is also a follower of human habitation and is commonly seen around homes. It spends the day in nooks and crannies and emerges at dusk to scour walls for insects, spiders, and small lizards. The tokay is one of the most vocal lizards and their ''to-kay'' call can be plainly heard at a hundred yards. Females are oviparous and as a rule lay 2 eggs at a time. These hatch after about 2 months' incubation.

117 HEMIDACTYLUS TURCICUS
Turkish gecko

Classification   Order Squamata, Family Gekkonidae.
Distribution   North Africa, islands and coastal regions of Mediterranean lands, southwestern Asia; introduced in southeastern United States.
Identification   This species has a large depressed head, and prominent lidless eyes with vertical pupils. The upper scales are small and granular; rows of white keeled tubercles accent back. The digits have rather small claws and are slightly widened at the tip, with two series of longitudinal adhesive pads on the lower surface. The back is a translucent tan, gray, or pink with some irregularly arranged black spots. There are several dark bands on the tail. Total length: 4–5½ in (10–14 cm).
Habitat   Under tree bark and palm fronds, cracks in dry walls, crevices in rocky outcrops.
Biology   Like many other members of the family, the Turkish gecko is quite agile and active at dusk and by night, frequently living in or around houses. It feeds on insects and spiders attracted to light. If attacked or disturbed, it readily sheds part of its tail. One or two months after breeding, eggs can be seen through the female's translucent belly skin. The 2–3 eggs are deposited in tree hollows or rock clefts.

118 PHELSUMA CEPEDIANA
Blue-tailed day gecko

Classification   Order Squamata, Family Gekkonidae.
Distribution   Mauritius and Reunion islands.
Identification   This strikingly colored gecko has large eyes with round pupils. Its dorsal scales are granular, while belly scales are smooth and overlapping. The toes have broad adhesive lamellae and lack claws. The basic coloration of the back is dark-green to turquoise, with numerous reddish marks of various shapes and patterns. There is a red stripe, in the form of an upside-down U, on the tip of the snout, extending from one eye to the other. Total length: 4½–5½ in (11–14 cm).
Habitat   Rainforests of hill and mountain regions.
Biology   The species is almost exclusively arboreal and, like other representatives of the genus *Phelsuma*, is active only by day. It feeds mainly on insects and normally moves around slowly and cautiously; but if attacked or threatened, it flees rapidly, climbing the trunks and branches of trees. Males are equipped with a good vocal apparatus and signal their presence, particularly in the breeding season, with strong, shrill calls. Females are oviparous and lay their 2–3 eggs under bark several times a year.

119 PHYLLURUS CORNUTUS
Northern leaf-tailed gecko

Classification   Order Squamata, Family Gekkonidae.
Distribution   Extreme eastern regions of Australia.
Identification   This gecko has a large, flat, triangular head, eyes with a vertical pupil, a fairly flattened body and a short and extremely broad leaf or shield-shaped tail ending in a short, slender, spiny tip. Its limbs are long and spindly. The sides of the head, the neck, the flanks and the upper surface of the tail are covered with long, spiny, pointed scales. The back is olive-green or brownish, with some large, transverse, black-bordered pale blotches. There are numerous dark streaks and reticulations on the head, the flanks and the legs. The belly is whitish. Total length: 6¼–9¾ in (16–25 cm).
Habitat   Coastal rainforests and adjacent sclerophyllous woodlands.
Biology   Nocturnally active, this arboreal gecko can be seen exploring large tree trunks as well as saplings for arthropods. Its unusual body shape and cryptic coloration greatly enhance its ability to camouflage itself and avoid predation. During the day it retreats under bark or into tree hollows.

120 PTYCHOZOON LIONOTUM
Gliding gecko

Classification   Order Squamata, Family Gekkonidae.
Distribution   Burma and Thailand.
Identification   This species has an extremely flattened body and is characterized by large folds of skin along the sides of the head, flanks, legs, and the tail. The digits of the feet are spatula-shaped and toes are interconnected to their tips by large membranes. The upper parts of the body are brown or gray-brown, with various dark spots and stripes on the back, as well as several transverse bands on the tail. Total length: 4½–6 in (11–15 cm).
Habitat   Tropical rainforests.
Biology   This gecko leads an exclusively arboreal life and is active only at night when it climbs or squats on trunks and branches, normally folding its broad flaps of skin along the sides of its body. Nevertheless it can escape a predator very quickly by hurling itself from the tree where it has settled and making short gliding flights. During flight, the legs and tail are spread wide and the folds of skin expand, functioning like a miniature parachute. The females are oviparous and lay their two eggs below the bark. They hatch after about 10 weeks' incubation.

121 TARENTOLA MAURITANICA
Moorish gecko

Classification   Order Squamata, Family Gekkonidae.
Distribution   Southern Europe and North Africa.
Identification   This Moorish gecko has a flat, triangular head, and eyes with a vertical pupil. The body is covered with small granular scales and ridged tubercles arranged in longitudinal rows. The digits are spatula-shaped and have adhesive pads along their entire length. Only the third and fourth toes have tiny claws. The back and tail are light brown or grayish, with a number of dark bands best developed on the tail. Total length: 4–6¼ in (10–16 cm).
Habitat   Olive groves, coastal pinewoods, dry walls, ruins, old buildings.
Biology   This species lives mainly on tree trunks and on walls of old buildings. It is active during the day in the cooler months and at night during the warm summer season. It is very agile and an adept climber and is often attracted to lights where insects have gathered. It is itself hunted by nocturnal raptors and snakes. The breeding season is in spring and mating is usually preceded by violent fights among the males. The females are oviparous and lay their eggs under tree bark or in the clefts of walls.

122 ANOLIS CAROLINENSIS
Green anole

Classification   Order Squamata, Family Iguanidae.
Distribution   Southeastern United States from southern Virginia to eastern Texas.
Identification   This lizard has a fairly long wedge-shaped head, slender body, and a very long, slender tail. Scales are tiny and granular and toes possess large pads. Usually green in color but can quickly change to dark brown. The males have a large, pink throat fan which can be fully expanded to advertise presence, during courtship, or in the course of territorial disputes. Total length: 5–8 in (13–20 cm).
Habitat   Thin, sunny woods, shrubby and bushy ground, walls of orchards and gardens.
Biology   The American "chameleon" is an extremely visually oriented lizard that communicates with others of its kind by a show of color and behavioral signals. Head-bobbing, body push-ups, open-mouth displays and flashing the throat fan warning are all part of the anoles' special signalling system. Their body color conveys changes in their body temperature, mood, or state of stress. The anole is arboreal and diurnally active. They slowly stalk small insects and spiders among shrubs, vines and on walls and window screens. During spring and summer months, females lay single eggs, every two weeks, in leaf litter and moist debris.

123 BASILISCUS PLUMIFRONS
Double-crested basilisk

Classification   Order Squamata, Family Iguanidae.
Distribution   Nicaragua, Costa Rica, and Panama.
Identification   Adult males have conspicuous high crests on their head, midline of back and tail. Females lack the crests. It is bright green with blue or yellowish spotting along flanks and crests; the iris of the eye is red. Total length: 18–28 in (46–70 cm).
Habitat   Tropical rainforests.
Biology   This diurnally active lizard lives almost entirely in trees and shrub tangles along river courses and swamps. In the dense vegetation, thanks to its cryptic coloration, it can safely devote itself to dining on insects, snails, fish, frogs, and small lizards as well as flowers and fruits. When forced to flee from a predator, this reptile may rear up on its hind legs and run away at remarkable speed, either over the ground or across short stretches of water. They also use water-walking in feeding activities. Because of their bipedal locomotion abilities on water they have been dubbed the Jesus Christ lizard. It is an egg layer, producing up to 20 eggs in a clutch, and nests several times each season.

---

124 CROTAPHYTUS COLLARIS
Collared lizard

Classification   Order Squamata, Family Iguanidae.
Distribution   South central United States, northern Mexico.
Identification   The collared lizard has a large, heavy head, a fairly stocky body and a long, thin tail. The hind legs are stronger and bigger than the forelegs. The basic color may be gray, blue-green, or yellowish, with numerous light ocelli on the back, tail and limbs, and several light transverse stripes on the flanks. There are two conspicuous black transverse bands on the neck which in shape resemble a collar. In adult males the throat is dark spotted and bluish-green or orange. Females have unspotted throats and develop reddish-orange bars on sides of neck and body during the breeding season. Total length: 8–14 in (20–35 cm).
Habitat   Dry, rocky ground with sparse vegetation.
Biology   This lizard frequents limestone ridges, rocky gullies, and boulder strewn mountain slopes where there are plenty of lookouts, good basking sites, and safe refuges. It is active mainly in the morning and bounds from rock top to rock top in search of insects and small lizards after warming in the sun. The adults are fiercely aggressive and will sometimes attack and bite adversaries of considerable size. But if cornered they prefer to flee rather than fight, rearing up on their hind legs and running off at high speed, using the tail as counter-balance.

125 CYCLURA CORNUTA
Rhinoceros iguana

Classification Order Squamata, Family Iguanidae.
Distribution Haiti and Dominican Republic.
Identification As its common name implies, this iguana has a large, heavy head, a sturdy body, strong legs and a long tail flattened from side to side. The vertebral line of the body bears a crest, composed of pointed horny scales, extending from the nape to the tip of the tail. Color is uniformly gray, brown or olive-brown. Males have three large, prominent and pointed tubercles, similar to small horns on their snout, an adipose pad in the form of a helmet on the occipital region of their head and a very large, pendulous throat pouch. Females have no helmet or horns. Total length: 28–48 in (71–120 cm).
Habitat Dry, rocky ground with cactuses and thorny bushes.
Biology The huge ''rhino'' iguana lives predominantly in rocky zones with little vegetative cover. It is active only by day and feeds almost wholly on plants and berries. The adults are shy and quite agile, fleeing rapidly into their burrows as soon as there is a hint of danger. When attacked by a predator, they nevertheless defend themselves with great determination, biting and striking the aggressor repeatedly with their strong tail. Egg laying females deposit 10–24 or more eggs while buried deep in the substrate. These hatch in about 15–17 weeks.

126 IGUANA IGUANA
Green iguana

Classification Order Squamata, Family Iguanidae.
Distribution Central America, northern regions of South America.
Identification A large, green, big-headed lizard with comb-like spines down the midline of the back and tail. The spines are best developed on the neck. A very large circular scale is present on the lower jaw below the ear and the throat has a jagged-edged dewlap. Males have better developed crests and larger heads with splashes of orange. Typical specimens are bright green or olive-green, with a number of dark transverse stripes on the flanks and tail. Total length: 40–79 in (100–200 cm).
Habitat Tropical rainforests.
Biology The green iguana is widely distributed in the tropical forests of Central and South America. It climbs tree trunks and branches with remarkable speed, and prefers densely vegetated areas along waterways. The young feed mainly on insects while the adults are almost exclusively vegetarian. Although capable of defending itself effectively by biting and striking out with the tail, the iguana normally chooses flight rather than battle, often seeking safety by throwing itself into the water and swimming off with great agility. Like most iguanids, *Iguana* is an egg-layer, producing 20–40 eggs per clutch. These hatch in 10–15 weeks.

127 PHRYNOSOMA SOLARE
Regal horned lizard

Classification Order Squamata, Family Iguanidae.
Distribution Arizona and northwestern Mexico.
Identification This iguanid has an extremely wide, flat body, short, sturdy legs and a short, slender tail. The head is crowned by 4 large, closely positioned spines. A single row of pointed scales fringe body. Some individuals have a light longitudinal stripe along the vertebral line of the body, extending from nape to tail. Total length: 3¼–6½ in (9–16 cm).
Habitat Arid and semiarid rocky terrain, upland desert.
Biology Active mainly in the morning and late afternoon, the "horny toad" spends the hottest part of the day inside a burrow dug in loose soil. It typically preys on ants and positions itself close to their trails or nest entrance. It is fairly agile and energetic, and if alarmed will bury itself with rapid body movements. If cornered, it becomes completely immobile, remaining stiff until all danger is past, sometimes squirting small drops of blood from the corner of its eye. One to two dozen eggs are laid in late summer.

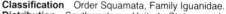

128 SAUROMALUS OBESUS
Chuckwalla

Classification Order Squamata, Family Iguanidae.
Distribution Southwestern United States and northwestern Mexico.
Identification A large, big-bellied lizard with loose folds of skin about its shoulders and neck. The skin on the back is covered with small but coarse granular scales. The base of the tail is thick and flattened, while the tip is thin and blunt. The upper body is dark gray or brownish. In males the head, chest, and legs are blackish, while the rest of the body is light gray or rusty and the tail is pale yellow. Females and young, by contrast, have broad, dark transverse bands across the back and tail. Total length: 11–16 in (28–41 cm).
Habitat Arid, stony desertscrub.
Biology "Chucks" are typically associated with rocky outcrops, old larvae flows, dry flats with scattered boulders and desertlands where creosote bush is common. It is exclusively diurnal and spends the morning and late afternoon hours perched on favorite rock basking spots. Its diet is mainly vegetarian, consisting of leaves, flowers and fruit. Despite its bulk, this lizard is quite agile and speedy; if attacked by a predator, it escapes quickly into a rock cleft, gulps air and firmly wedges itself in the crevice. Their clutch of 5–16 eggs is laid in summer.

129 SCELOPORUS GRACIOSUS
Sagebrush lizard

Classification Order Squamata, Family Iguanidae.
Distribution Western United States and northern Baja California.
Identification This spiny lizard has a heavy, slightly flattened head and a stout body completely covered by keeled, pointed, overlapping scales. The upper body is grayish or greenish-brown, with dark spotting and crossbars. Pale stripes are on the upper sides, a black bar is often present on the shoulders, and the front leg pocket is usually rusty colored. In males the throat is mottled pale blue and the sides of the belly are darker blue, while females are orange on flanks and neck. Total length: 4¾–6 in (12–15 cm).
Habitat Dry bushlands into oak-juniper and pine-fir forestlands.
Biology This small "scelop" is a commonly encountered reptile in Sagebrush country. It never strays far from rocky retreats, burrows, or brushy thicket in which it habitually finds refuge when alarmed. In the morning, after basking in the sun, it starts hunting for food, consisting mainly of insects and spiders. Courtship and copulation, preceded by sparring among rival males occur in spring; June–August each female lays one or two clutches of 2–8 eggs in a shallow earthen cavity.

130 UTA STANSBURIANA
Side-blotched lizard

Classification Order Squamata, Family Iguanidae.
Distribution Western United States and northwestern Mexico.
Identification As its common name implies, this small lizard has a characteristic large spot, bluish-black in color, on each side of its chest behind the front leg. A fold with granular scales crosses the throat. Scales on the back are small, smooth, and lack spines. The color of the back is gray to black, or yellowish to dark brown, with or without speckles, stripes, and blotches. In some populations, males are speckled with pale blue. Total length: 4–6¼ in (10–16 cm).
Habitat Arid or semiarid terrain with low plant or scattered tree growth.
Biology Strictly diurnal and ground-dwelling, this abundant small iguanid lives on a wide variety of dry terrains where the plant cover is usually sparse. In order to be fully active it must have a fairly high body temperature, and when it emerges from its nocturnal shelter it warms up for a long time before it begins its foraging activity. They are insectivores. Populations which live in northern parts of the range become inactive in the winter, while those in southern areas are active throughout the year. The breeding and egg laying season is in spring and summer. Depending on locality, females may lay 1–7 clutches of 1–8 eggs in a given season.

131 LACERTA AGILIS
Sand lizard

Classification Order Squamata, Family Lacertidae.
Distribution Europe (except much of Iberian peninsula, Italy, and Mediterranean islands), western and central Asia.
Identification This lizard has a fairly broad and short-snouted head, and a stocky body supported by relatively short limbs. The tail is about 1½ times the body length. A distinct band of narrow scales is present along the back's mid-line. The basic coloration is green, gray, or brownish, with a wide dark band down the center of the back marked with a longitudinal series of dark spots or blotches. A series of similar marks is often found on the flanks. Males have a distinctly larger head and typically have greenish flanks; females have brownish flanks with pattern well defined on flanks. Total length: 7–10 in (18–25 cm).
Habitat Coastal dunes, hedgerows, woodland edge, fields, and urban gardens.
Biology The sand lizard is commonly seen along sun-drenched park paths, roadsides, and in sandy heathland, where it searches out insects and spiders during the morning and late afternoon hours. Although fond of basking, it avoids the midday sun and may appear to be quite rare during the hottest days of summer. Abandoned rodent tunnels or self-dug retreats under a root clump are used to escape the summer heat and winter's chill. Mating occurs in spring and females deposit their 3–14 peanut-sized eggs in early summer.

132 LACERTA LEPIDA
Ocellated lizard

Classification Order Squamata, Family Lacertidae.
Distribution Iberian peninsula, southern France, extreme northwestern Italy, and northwestern Africa.
Identification Europe's largest lizard. This species has a broad, massive head, a robust body with powerful hind legs, and a whip-like tail which is half to twice the body length. Adults are generally green, brown or grayish, with fine black-ish reticulations on the back and large black-bordered blue spots on the flanks. The olive or grayish young are marked with many black-edged whitish ocelli. The males have a larger head than the females and during the breeding season take on a particularly bright livery. Total length: 16–32 in (40–81 cm).
Habitat Scrublands, open woods, old olive groves, thickets, rocky slopes.
Biology This large sun-loving lizard's preferred habitat is dry, rocky terrain with scrubby plant cover. Largely terrestrial, it is extremely agile and speedy, and is active much of the day. It feeds mainly on insects but often hunts small lizards and young mammals and birds. The males are territorial and during the spring breeding period are highly aggressive to-ward rival males. About 40 days after mating, females deposit 6–16 eggs in a tree hollow or shallow earthern cavity. These hatch after 3 months' incubation.

133 LACERTA VIVIPARA
Viviparous lizard

Classification Order Squamata, Family Lacertidae.
Distribution Europe (excluding southern regions and Mediterranean islands), southern Asia.
Identification This small-headed, blunt-snouted lizard has an elongated body and fairly short legs. The thickish tail is longer than the rest of the body. Color and pattern are quite variable. Most specimens are brownish or olive. The males, characterized by a reddish belly, have numerous small spots on the back and flanks. The females have a white, yellow or dark mustard-colored belly, a backstripe, and often thin light-colored streaks on either side of the back. Total length: 6–7 in (15–18 cm).
Habitat Alpine meadows, woodland edges, marshes, bogs, moors.
Biology The viviparous lizard is an inhabitant of cool, humid regions and is frequently encountered near water. They often have a favorite basking site on a log, stump, or rocky perch and return to it day after day to warm themselves. When they reach their "preferred body temperature" they are very alert and ready to pursue spiders and small insects. Most populations are ovoviviparous and females give birth to 2–12 young at a time.

134 PODARCIS MURALIS
Common wall lizard

Classification Order Squamata, Family Lacertidae.
Distribution Western, central-eastern and southern Europe, northwestern Asia Minor.
Identification Superficially like the viviparous lizard, the wall lizard has a rather flattened body, comparatively long head with pointed snout, and long legs. Color and pattern are extremely variable. Typical representatives are brown, gray or greenish. The back of the males is covered with blackish, blotching reticulations, or there may be a dark stripe along the vertebral line and numerous light markings on the flanks. The female's back is lighter and she normally displays two thin light-colored bands along the sides of the back and dark flanks. The belly may be whitish, yellow or, at least in some males, reddish, with scattered black flecks. Total length: 6–9 in (15–23 cm).
Habitat Rocky slopes, dry walls, ruins, margins of woods, scrubland.
Biology An exploiter of vertical surfaces, this lizard climbs with great agility on sheer rock faces, building walls, and tree trunks; occasionally it will make long leaps and will not hesitate to dive into water to escape capture. It is active only by day, feeds on insects and small spiders, and is in turn hunted by weasels, shrews, birds, other lizards, and snakes. Large colonies are sometimes encountered in ideal habitat.

135 PSAMMODROMUS ALGIRUS
Sand lizard, Algerian sand lizard

Classification   Order Squamata, Family Lacertidae.
Distribution   Northwest Africa, Iberian peninsula, southern France, and island of Lampedusa.
Identification   This lizard has a slender body and a very long, stiff tail. Its back and flank scales are large, flat, and pointed and bear a prominent keel. Like the belly scales, they overlap strongly. The dorsal color is deep metallic brown with two light bands along the sides of the back which extend from the rear of the head to the tail. The flanks are darker than the back and display a light longitudinal stripe. The males have one or two blue ocelli in the shoulder region, and during the breeding season, the throat and the sides of the head turn orange. Total length: 7—12 in (18—30 cm).
Habitat   Coastal pinewoods, evergreen oak forest, Mediterranean scrublands, and woodlots with dense undergrowth.
Biology   This species is active only by day and normally lives among thickets and brambles where it hunts among the leaf litter for arthropod prey. It digs its own burrow at the foot of trees and shrubs and ventures out on to open ground only to warm its body. It is very common in parts of its range, but because of its densely vegetated habitat, cryptic coloration and secretive habitats, it is rarely seen. It is extremely agile and speedy, and when attacked reacts by viciously biting its aggressor and letting out high-pitched squeals. The adults mate in spring and the females lay eggs in early summer.

136 TAKYDROMUS SEXLINEATUS
Oriental long-tailed lizard

Classification   Order Squamata, Family Lacertidae.
Distribution   Southern China, Indochina, Malaccan peninsula, Sumatra.
Identification   This slender-bodied species has an extraordinarily well-developed tail which may measure three to five times the length of the body. The legs are rather well developed; toes are long and slender. The back and belly are covered with large, strongly keeled scales, the keels forming continuous longitudinal rows. It is olive to reddish brown with two light lines along the sides of the back which extend from the tip of the snout to the tail. The flanks are darker than the back, with a light longitudinal stripe. Total length: 8—14 in (20—36 cm).
Habitat   Open, sunny grassland.
Biology   This species is found in meadows and on grassy slopes, and is active mainly in the morning and late afternoon. It eats insects and spiders and moves through the grass by clinging to the tops of stalks and leaping from plant to plant. The very long tail distributes the animal's weight over a number of stems and makes it easier for it to flee, flinging itself onto the softest vegetation. The females are oviparous and normally lay 1—4 eggs during the summer.

137 CHALCIDES CHALCIDES
Three-toed skink

Classification Order Squamata, Family Scincidae.
Distribution Northwest Africa, Iberian peninsula, southern France, Italy, Sardinia and Sicily.
Identification This species has a serpentine body, covered with smooth, glossy scales, and a small head that is hardly distinguishable from the body. The tail tip ends in a sharp, horny point. The limbs are extremely small, with just three tiny toes. Its coloration is quite variable – brown, olive or bronze. Animals living in the west of the range have 9–13 dark longitudinal stripes on back and flanks, while those from the east and south have 4–6 thin dark bands along the sides of the back. Total length: 8–16½ in (20–42 cm).
Habitat Grassy slopes and sunny meadows near water.
Biology The three-toed skink lives almost entirely in areas with low but lush vegetation. It uses its tiny legs only to crawl slowly over the ground in search of earthworms, slugs, and small insects, but when alarmed makes off rapidly with snake-like movements, keeping its legs tucked into its sides. It dislikes the cold and enters its deep underground retreat in October and does not reappear on the surface until the first warm days of the following spring. The females are ovoviviparous and give birth to 3–20 young during the summer.

138 CHALCIDES OCELLATUS
Ocellated skink

Classification Order Squamata, Family Scincidae.
Distribution Sardinia, Sicily, Malta, Greece, Crete, and northern Africa into southwestern Asia.
Identification The species has a small pointed head, a thick neck, a rather stout cylindrical body supported by short legs with five-toed feet, and a tail which is about half, or less, of the animal's total length. Its smooth, glossy scales, are gray or light brown with numerous black, white-centered spots arranged in irregular crossbands. In some individuals the body displays two light stripes along the sides of the back which are bordered by a dark band on the flank. Total length: 6–12 in (15–30 cm).
Habitat Scrublands behind beaches, grassy slopes, dry, sandy-soiled fields.
Biology A fast-moving, agile reptile, the ocellated skink is active mainly in the early morning and late afternoon. It uses its wedge-shaped snout and strong legs to dig long under-ground tunnels at the foot of trees, where it finds refuge from a pursuing predator. It feeds principally on insects and spiders. The adults may mate several times a year. The females are ovoviviparous and give birth to 3–11 young.

139 EUMECES ALGERIENSIS
Berber's skink

Classification Order Squamata, Family Scincidae.
Distribution Northwest Africa.
Identification The species has a rather heavy head, a fairly stout body on strong legs with five-toed feet, and a stocky tail which is slightly longer than the rest of the body. The upper parts are covered with smooth, overlapping scales and are brown with various orange or reddish crossbands. The underside is uniformly white or yellowish. Total length: 12–16½ in (30–42 cm).
Habitat Dry agriculture and semiarid rocky regions with plenty of grass and shrub cover, Mediterranean scrublands.
Biology This large skink prefers open, sunny ground near areas with low, tangled vegetation. It digs particularly deep burrows in which it takes refuge for the night and during the hottest parts of the day. Despite its heavy build it is a very agile animal. When alarmed, it flees rapidly to hide under large stones or in the dense scrub. It surfaces mainly in the morning and late afternoon, when it hunts for food, principally snails and insects. The female provides brood care by encircling her 3–20 eggs with her body to protect them for their two-month incubation period. The hatchlings are independent.

140 EUMECES FASCIATUS
Five-lined skink

Classification Order Squamata, Family Scincidae.
Distribution Southeastern Canada and eastern United States.
Identification This skink, with its fairly slender body and short legs with five-toed feet, is particularly handsome. The upper surfaces are glossy brown or black, with five broad light-colored longitudinal stripes extending from the head to the tail. The stripes disappear in older animals and adults may be uniformly brown. In the young the tail is bright blue, and in courting males the chin and jaws turn bright red-orange. Total length: 4¾–8 in (12–20 cm).
Habitat Clearings or edges of hardwood forests, pine barrens, old woodlots, wet hammocks, suburban gardens.
Biology This skink is frequently seen scurrying about leaf litter in woods or around lush foundation plantings. In the morning, after emerging from its burrow, it warms up in the sun on a fallen tree trunk or a rotting stump and, when it has reached optimal body temperature, sets off in search of insects, spiders, earthworms, and small lizards. Breeding occurs in the spring and mating is preceded by violent fights between rival males. The females lay 6–12 eggs in late spring or early summer and remain encircled about them until they hatch.

141 MABUYA STRIATA
African striped skink

Classification   Order Squamata, Family Scincidae.
Distribution   East and southern Africa.
Identification   The species has a small head hardly distinguishable from the trunk, tiny eyes, and a window in each of its lower eyelids. The body is covered with extremely glossy overlapping scales with fine keels. There are spiny scales on the soles of the feet. Back coloration is variable and may be pale gray, reddish-brown, dark brown or black with two light stripes along the sides of the back which extend from the snout to the tail, passing above the eyes. In adults these stripes are hardly noticeable and sometimes the color of the back is uniformly dark brown or blackish. Total length: 7–10 in (18–25 cm).
Habitat   Mangrove swamp edges to dry savannas and semiarid woodlands.
Biology   Striped skinks are diurnally active and are commonly seen around houses in towns and villages where they quickly become accustomed to human activity. They are mainly arboreal but also live on rocky outcrops. They forage on a wide variety of invertebrates. In the southern and cooler part of its range, females give birth to 3–9 young in summer. Populations in warmer climates may reproduce year round.

---

142 SCINCUS SCINCUS
Sand skink

Classification   Order Squamata, Family Scincidae.
Distribution   Desert regions of North Africa.
Identification   It has a long, wedge-shaped snout with countersunk lower jaw and a tapering body completely covered with shiny, closely juxtaposed scales. The legs are short and sturdy, while the toes are long and flattened, edged with fringes of projecting scales. The tail is short and stocky, terminating in a thin point. The sand skink is yellowish or yellowish-brown, with several brownish or black crossbands. Total length: 7–8 in (18–20 cm).
Habitat   Sandy deserts.
Biology   This ''sandfish'' is wholly adapted to life in arid sandy zones and spends much of its time digging long galleries in the soft dunes. If surprised on the surface by a predator, it buries itself with astonishing speed in the sand with swift, slithering movements. Active mainly in the morning, it feeds on locusts and beetles, and is in turn hunted by the desert monitor (*Varanus griseus*) and certain snakes. The females are ovoviviparous and give birth to 2–10 young at a time, each only about an inch and a half long.

143 TILIQUA SCINCOIDES
Blue-tongued skink

Classification Order Squamata, Family Scincidae.
Distribution Northern, eastern and southeastern Australia.
Identification This skink has a large head, a long and heavily built body and short legs with five toes. The conical tail is about 50–75 percent of the length of the rest of the body. The tongue is fairly large with a characteristic blue color. Scales are smooth and overlapping. The upper surfaces are silvery-gray to brown with a series of dark wide crossbands. The belly and throat are uniformly white, gray, or yellowish. Total length: 14–22 in (36–56 cm).
Habitat Coastal woodlands to montane forests and into interior grasslands.
Biology This ground-dwelling lizard is active by day and often shelters in a hollow log or under woodland debris at night. It is normally slow and sluggish in its movements, but should danger occur it will escape quite rapidly. If cornered, it will stand its ground, open its mouth wide, display its blue tongue, and hiss. It feeds principally on insects and gastropods, often supplementing its diet with berries and flowers of various plants. The females are ovoviviparous and give birth to 5–25 young at a time.

144 CNEMIDOPHORUS SEXLINEATUS
Six-lined race runner

Classification Order Squamata, Family Teiidae.
Distribution Central and eastern United States.
Identification This streamlined lizard has a long whip-like tail. Its dorsal scales are tiny and granular while the belly scales are smooth and rectangular, and the tail is distinctly whorled with rough scales. The back has 6 or 7 light stripes which are separated by solid greenish to black bands. The belly is white with bluish tints. In males the throat is green or blue, in females white. Total length: 6–10½ in (15–27 cm).
Habitat Dry, sunny prairie hillsides, thicket edges, sandy floodplains, dunes.
Biology Ground-dwelling and wholly diurnal, this lizard is agile, speedy, and very wary, usually fleeing at the slightest alarm and hiding in dense vegetation or in rodents' burrows. It spends the early hours of the day on rocks or stones, exposed to the warming sun, and when it has reached optimal body temperature sets off in search of food, comprised mainly of insects. The breeding period is spring and early summer; each female lays 1–6 eggs and these hatch after 1–2 months' incubation.

145 TUPINAMBIS TEGUIXIN
Common tegu

Classification   Order Squamata, Family Teiidae.
Distribution   South America, east of the Andes.
Identification   One of the biggest lizards in South America, its large head is covered with large regular plates, and its sturdy body is supported by powerful legs. The rounded tail is considerably longer than the rest of the body and the latter half is banded. Its dorsal scales are granular, those ventrally are larger and rectangular. Typical specimens are dark brown or black with groups of small white or yellowish spots arranged in crossbands. Total length: 30–56 in (76–142 cm).
Habitat   Tropical woodlands and forests.
Biology   The tegu lives in regions of dense, luxuriant plant growth and is often encountered in tracts of forest bordering rivers. They also have a tendency to follow human habitation and often thrive at edge of villages. While largely terrestrial, they are good climbers and swim well. A voracious reptile, it eats both invertebrates and small vertebrates, occasionally visiting cultivated areas to kill chickens and steal their eggs. Very wary, it flees rapidly at the slightest alarm, but when attacked it will put up a fight and can inflict very painful bites and powerful blows with its tail. The females are oviparous and generally lay their 4–8 eggs in large termite mounds. The termites securely seal in the eggs thus protecting them from desiccation and predators during their incubation period.

---

146 VARANUS GOULDI
Gould's monitor

Classification   Order Squamata, Family Varanidae.
Distribution   Australia.
Identification   This species has a relatively flat head with small scales, a very long neck and a fairly slender but robust body. The limbs are heavy and the feet are furnished with long, sharp claws. The tail is very long, flattened laterally, and ends in a thin point, the last several inches of which are white or yellow. Coloration is extremely variable, ranging from yellowish to dark brown or black, with numerous light and dark streaks and spots which usually tend to be arranged in narrow, irregular crossbands across the back. A well defined black stripe usually passes through the eye and crosses the temporal region. The legs are covered with fine white or yellow spots. Total length: 39–68 in (100–160 cm).
Habitat   Coastal sclerophyllous woodland, semiarid grass and bushlands, sandy deserts.
Biology   Gould's monitor inhabits a very wide variety of environments. It spends the night in deep underground burrows and is active mainly in the morning when, after warming up in the sun, it goes hunting for food. It is a skillful predator, hunting birds, mammals and reptiles. Large individuals will rear up on their hind legs to defend themselves and to survey surrounding territory. The females are oviparous.

147 VARANUS KOMODOENSIS
Komodo dragon

Classification   Order Squamata, Family Varanidae.
Distribution   Indonesian islands of Komodo, Rintja, Padar and Flores.
Identification   This gigantic reptile has a large heavy head, a massive body, powerful legs with large sharp clawed feet, and a long, laterally compressed tail. Its tongue is very long, slender, and deeply forked. The body is covered with round or oval scales and its color is uniformly dark gray or brownish-black. Adults may measure more than 10 ft (3 m) in length and weigh up to 310 pounds (140 kg), and are thus the largest living saurians.
Habitat   Woodland thickets, forest fringes and clearings.
Biology   The Komodo dragon is a strong and fearsome predator which, on the islands where it lives, virtually occupies those ecological niches left vacant by large carnivorous mammals. To attack and kill the wild pigs, deer and birds on which it feeds, the reptile uses its powerful, curved claws and strong jaws with shark-like teeth. Victims are usually taken by ambush. Those which are bitten and escape are carefully trailed using its tongue to pick up chemical signals given off by the prey. When large prey is killed, several individuals share in the feast, but only the bigger animals get the choicest portions. Despite their size they are quite agile and good tree climbers and swimmers. Females lay several clutches of about 18 eggs per year.

148 VARANUS NILOTICUS
Nile monitor

Classification   Order Squamata, Family Varanidae.
Distribution   Much of sub-Saharan Africa.
Identification   Largest of African lizards, it is quickly recognized by its stout body, powerful limbs with sharply clawed feet, and its long, laterally compressed, pale banded tail. The back is grayish-brown to olive-brown, with numerous yellowish spots arranged in regular crossbands. Juveniles are brightly patterned in black and bright yellow. Total length: 39–84 in (100–213 cm).
Habitat   Sandy and tree-covered banks of rivers and lakes.
Biology   The Nile monitor is a largely aquatic reptile which spends the early hours of the day on rocky outcrops, tree stumps, or islets of sand or mud, warming up in the sun; having reached optimal body temperature, it goes hunting for food. This active and voracious predator feeds on crabs, mussels, frogs, fish, reptiles and birds. As a rule, if danger threatens, it dives into the water, quickly disappearing among the bottom vegetation; but when cornered by an aggressor it boldly fights back, biting and lashing out with its tail. The females are oviparous and lay their 29–60 eggs in large termite mounds where they incubate at fairly constant humidity and temperature for 4–6 months. Young emerge from the nest after summer rains have softened the covering.

149 ACROCHORDUS JAVANICUS
Javan wart snake

Classification   Order Squamata, Family Acrochordidae.
Distribution   Cambodia, coastal Southeast Asia, through the Indo-Malaysian archipelago to Australia.
Identification   This flabby skinned snake has a small head hardly distinguishable from the body, with tiny eyes and nostrils located very close together high on the snout. The head, body and tail are covered with finely keeled and pointed granular scales which have a sandpaper-like texture. The tail is prehensile. Dorsal color varies from gray to dark brown with broad dark crossbands or reticulations fusing to form a vertebral band. Total length: 55–100 in (140–254 cm).
Habitat   Freshwater streams and rivers and associated estuaries, brackish lagoons, canals.
Biology   The "file" or "elephant trunk" snake has markedly aquatic habits and lives mainly in delta regions, sometimes even venturing into inlets of the sea. It can remain submerged for long periods and when obliged to replenish its stocks of oxygen only raises the part of the snout with the nostrils above the surface. It anchors its tail to roots or aquatic plants and remains hidden most of the day. At twilight it abandons its shelter to hunt for fish. The females are livebearing and give birth to 20–30 young at a time.

150 CYLINDROPHUS RUFUS
Red-tailed pipe snake

Classification   Order Squamata, Family Aniliidae.
Distribution   Widespread in Southeast Asia and the Indo-Australian archipelago.
Identification   The cylindrical body is covered with smooth, glossy scales; the flat blunt-snouted head is not distinct from the body; the eyes are tiny. The tail is very short and its tip is flattened. The upper surfaces are lavender-purple to black with gray-white transverse bars or crossbands. The underside of the tail is bright red. Total length: 28–36 in (71–91 cm).
Habitat   Rainforest clearings, mudflats, swamp edges, cultivated areas.
Biology   This snake has burrowing habits and lives almost exclusively on soft, wet ground where it digs long and often fairly deep tunnels. It is commonly encountered along waterways, drainage ditches, rice paddies, and gardens where it hides under rocks, rotted logs, or debris. It surfaces very rarely and then only during the night or after heavy rain. Favorite prey consists of small worm snakes of the genus *Typhlops*, but occasionally it also feeds on earthworms and insect larvae. When surprised above ground by an aggressor, it conceals its head beneath its coils and at the same time raises its tail so as to display the bright red color underneath. This species is a live-bearer, giving birth to 2–12 seven-inch long young at a time.

151 BOA CONSTRICTOR
Boa constrictor

Classification Order Squamata, Family Boidae.
Distribution Central and South America, from Mexico to northern Argentina.
Identification This gigantic snake has a large, heavy head and relatively small eyes with a vertical pupil. The body is covered with smooth, shiny scales. Its pattern is rather variable. Normally the ground color is pale brown or grayish, with a series of large interconnected reddish-brown rhomboidal blotches marking the back. The touching rhomboids encircle large lighter-colored ovals seen along the midline of the back. The tail coloration is sometimes striking and contrasts with the more somber colored body. Total length: 6–18½ ft (1.8–5.6 m).
Habitat Dry, semiarid llanos and savannas to cloud forests.
Biology The boa constrictor is active almost exclusively at dusk and at night. It is fairly sedentary, when not driven by hunger, sometimes remaining in the same spot for a number of days. Those in dry or colder environments may have periods of inactivity which last for several weeks. They seek shelter in tree hollows, rotted logs, or in mammal burrows. Boas prey on a wide variety of birds and mammals. Young, perhaps 20–60 in a litter, are born live and average about 18 inches in length. Small boas are somewhat arboreal and often forage in shrubs. As they grow larger and heavier, their movements become much more terrestrial.

---

152 CORALLUS CANINUS
Emerald tree boa

Classification Order Squamata, Family Boidae.
Distribution Amazon Basin.
Identification This species has a large and rather flat head, and small eyes with a vertical pupil. Deep pits are present in its lip scales. The body is flattened from side to side, triangular in cross-section, and the tail is short and prehensile. As in other Boidae, there are two tiny spurs at the sides of the cloacal opening. Its bright green color is patterned with numerous white crossbands. The yellow belly color extends onto the upper lips. Young are reddish-brown. Total length: 3–6½ ft (.9–2 m).
Habitat Tropical forests, lush vegetation bordering waterways, swamps, and marshes.
Biology The emerald tree boa has strictly arboreal habits and seldom descends to the ground. Its laterally flattened body and prehensile tail allow it to move nimbly through the foliage of trees and bushes. When resting, it grips a branch firmly with its tail and distributes the coils of its body evenly on either side. It feeds mainly on lizards and birds using the temperature-sensitive pits in its lip scales to help aim the strike. Long fang-like front teeth seize the prey which are constricted in its powerful coils. The females are ovoviviparous and give birth to 10–18 young at a time.

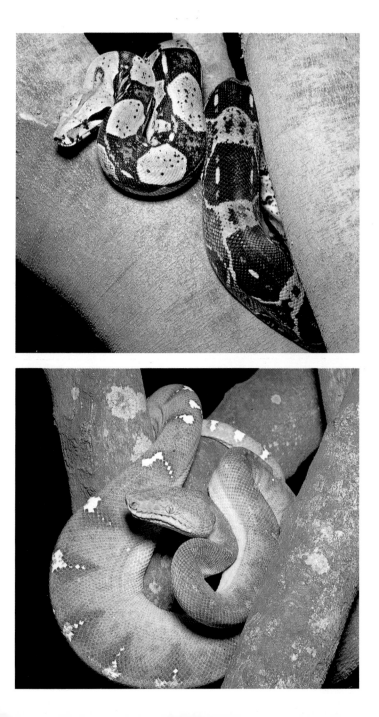

153 EPICRATES CENCHRIA
Rainbow boa

Classification Order Squamata, Family Boidae.
Distribution Central and South America, from Costa Rica to Argentina.
Identification It has a large head clearly distinguished from the trunk, small eyes with a vertical pupil and a fairly heavy body covered with smooth, dazzling iridescent scales. Although quite variable through their range, all are some shade of red, orange, or brown, and patterned with ring-like blotches or eyespots on their flanks. A series of connected dark rings may be present along its midline. Total length: 3–7 ft (.9–2.1 m).
Habitat Tropical forests, savannas.
Biology Rainbow boas are usually seen near water and seem to be attracted to the edge habitat around small rural villages. Although its tail is prehensile, it normally lives and hunts on the ground. It is active at dusk and by night, killing small mammals and birds by suffocating them between its coils. After a gestation of four or five months, females give birth to 8–20 young.

---

154 EUNECTES MURINUS
Anaconda

Classification Order Squamata, Family Boidae.
Distribution Tropical South America east of the Andes.
Identification The anaconda is probably the heaviest living snake. The head is quite large, the eyes are small with a vertical pupil, the nostrils open on top of the snout, the cylindrical body is covered with small glossy scales and the tail is fairly short. The backside is olive-gray or brownish-green, with one or two rows of large ovoid black spots across the back. A longitudinal series of large yellowish ocelli runs along the flanks. Total length: 10–30 ft (3–9 m).
Habitat Sluggish streams and rivers, marshes, and swamps.
Biology Unlike other Boidae, the "water boa" is strongly tied to aquatic habitats. An excellent swimmer, it can remain submerged for long periods and normally spends the day hidden among the plants on the bed of rivers or basking on a snag over water where it can quickly retreat. It hunts at twilight and night. Although fish and small to medium-sized birds and mammals are usually taken, large specimens will eat capybara, small tapir, and even caiman and crocodiles. The captured prey is suffocated by the powerful coils and swallowed head-first. Anacondas are live-bearers, giving birth to 10–50 two-to-three foot-long babies.

155 PYTHON MOLURUS
Asian rock python

Classification   Order Squamata, Family Boidae.
Distribution   West Pakistan, India, Sri Lanka, Burma, eastward through southern Asia to southeastern China.
Identification   This is one of the largest living snakes. Like other Boidae, it has a fairly big head, a heavy body covered with small iridescent scales, and two spurs, minute vestiges of hind legs, at the sides of the cloacal opening. Large reddish-brown to dark brown quadrangular blotches, outlined in cream or gold, run along the vertebral line of the pale tan or gray body. Each flank displays a series of light-centered blotches. There is a light colored lance-shaped patch on the head. Total length: 9–20 ft (2.7–6 m).
Habitat   Rocky hillsides, river valleys, dense forests, and clearings.
Biology   This snake is mainly active at twilight and at night, normally living in habitat close to water. It is an excellent climber and is sometimes seen basking in a snag at the top of a tree. It occasionally ventures into cultivated fields near villages and towns. Diet includes rodents, birds, reptiles and also farmyard animals. The females are oviparous and after laying their 1–3 dozen eggs, they encircle them with their body, staying to tend them until they hatch.

156 BOIGA DENDROPHILA
Mangrove snake

Classification   Order Squamata, Family Colubridae.
Distribution ·Thailand and Malay Peninsula to the Indo-Australian archipelago, Philippines.
Identification   Characterized by its large eyes with vertical pupils and a strongly compressed body covered with smooth, glossy scales, this satiny black snake is marked with narrow bright yellow bands. The large lip scales are also yellow and edged in black. Total length: 6–8 ft (1.8–2.4 m).
Habitat   Rainforest edge, mangrove swamps.
Biology   This mildly venomous, rear-fanged snake lives in the foliage of trees overhanging streams and rivers. It climbs with great agility and at night goes hunting for the various species of frogs, lizards, snakes, birds and small mammals that make up its diet. Prey is immobilized by their venom injected with the grooved teeth in the rear of the upper jaw. Bites are not considered dangerous to man. The females are oviparous, and the incubation period of the 7–10 egg clutch is about 3 months.

157 COLUBER VIRIDIFLAVUS
Western whip snake

Classification   Order Squamata, Family Colubridae.
Distribution   Northeastern Spain, southern France, southern Switzerland, northwestern Yugoslavia, Italy, Sicily, Malta, Corsica, Sardinia.
Identification   Well named, it has a small elongated head with prominent eyes, a fairly slim body and a long, finely tapering tail. Scales are smooth and have a polished look. In adults inhabiting the western and central regions of the range, it is greenish-yellow or yellowish, with numerous large dark crossbands which, on the rear half of the body and on the tail, are gradually transformed into longitudinal stripes. In the southern and northeastern regions of the range the adults are completely melanistic. Total length: 3–6½ ft (.9–2 m).
Habitat   Dry Mediterranean scrublands, rocky hillsides, open woodlands and thickets, ruins, occasionally damp meadows.
Biology   Fond of basking, this diurnally active snake is very alert after sunning and quick to flee. It is quite agile and speedy, living as a rule on the ground but occasionally climbing nimbly over rocks, shrubs, and bushes. A sight-hunter, it pursues startled lizards, snakes and small mammals. It is rather irritable and when molested often strikes out at the aggressor, trying repeatedly to bite it. Male precourtship rivalries are intense in the spring. Females lay 5–15 eggs during the summer and young hatch in about 2 months.

158 CORONELLA AUSTRIACA
Smooth snake

Classification   Order Squamata, Family Colubridae.
Distribution   Europe, Turkey, northern Iran.
Identification   This species has a small, moderately flattened head, and tiny eyes with round pupils. Body scales are smooth and highly polished. The backside is brown, grayish, or pinkish, with pairs of dark spots running down the middle of the back, which sometimes merge to form a series of crossbands. A thin dark line is present on the sides of the head, extending from the nostril, through the eye, onto the neck. Total length: 20–36 in (51–92 cm).
Habitat   Dry rocky hillsides, brushy slopes, dry evergreen and deciduous woodlands, sandy heathlands.
Biology   In parts of its range it is often mistaken for the asp viper or the long-nosed viper and frequently killed. The smooth snake frequents dry, sunny terrain, and is typically encountered around rock walls, quarries, railway embankments, vineyards, heaths and farm fields. Although it is active during the day, it does not like to bask fully exposed to the sun and its movements are secretive. It feeds on small lizards and young snakes, normally killing the prey by suffocating it with its coils. The females are ovoviviparous and give birth to 2–15 young at a time.

159 DASYPELTIS SCABRA
African egg-eating snake

Classification   Order Squamata, Family Colubridae.
Distribution   North Africa (excluding entire Saharan area), central and southern Africa.
Identification   The species has a small but elongated head with a rounded snout, hardly distinguishable from the trunk, eyes with a vertical pupil and a fairly slender body. The flank scales are small and have serrated keels. The tail is quite short. The back is gray, brownish-gray, or olive-brown with a median series of large, dark rhomboidal blotches flanked by narrow, irregular-shaped, dark, transverse bars. Two V-shaped marks are on the top of the head and a similar marking is seen on the nape of the neck. Total length: 20–46 in (50–116 cm).
Habitat   Dry scrublands to moist woodlands.
Biology   Similar in shape and color to the dangerous African night adder, *Causus rhombeatus*, the egg-eating snake is actually a completely harmless and inoffensive species where humans are concerned. It is active at night and moves with considerable agility and confidence both on rock faces and among the foliage of trees and bushes. It feeds exclusively on birds' eggs and can swallow eggs with a diameter three times the size of its head. When an egg reaches its throat, projections extending from the backbone into the snakes' gullet pierce the egg. Its contents are swallowed and the collapsed shell is regurgitated. Females lay 6–25 eggs in summer.

160 DISPHOLIDUS TYPUS
Boomslang

Classification   Order Squamata, Family Colubridae.
Distribution   Sub-Saharan Africa.
Identification   A large snake with a distinct head bearing large eyes with round pupils. Its body scales are keeled. Males are brightly colored: leaf-green with light green belly, yellow with black-edged scales and a speckled head, black with black-edged gray belly scales, or red with an orangish-pink belly. Females are brown or olive with a white to brown belly. Total length: 4–6½ ft (1.2–2 m).
Habitat   Savannas, bush country, and open forests.
Biology   The boomslang is an arboreal and diurnally active snake. It has excellent vision and it moves nimbly up trunks or through the foliage in pursuit of lizards and birds. It is not aggressive by nature, but when cornered, inflates its neck to show off its brightly colored skin. It does not hesitate to strike. It ejects a small amount of potent venom which attacks blood cells and prevents clotting. Although envenomation is rare, successful bites are highly dangerous to humans. Boomslangs are egg-layers and 10–25 eggs are deposited in leaf litter or a tree hollow in summer.

161 ELAPHE LONGISSIMA
Aesculapian snake

Classification Order Squamata, Family Colubridae.
Distribution Central, southern and eastern Europe, northern Turkey, and northern Iran.
Identification The adults of this large slender, smooth-scaled species are olive and gray-brown often with small white spots on scale edges. In some individuals there are a pair of longitudinal stripes on each side of the back. A dark streak behind the eye, followed by a muted yellow blotch, are usually seen. Young have rows of dark spots on the body and vivid head markings. Total length: 3–6½ ft (.9–2 m).
Habitat Dry, sunny wooded slopes, forest edges and clearings, meadows.
Biology Fond of stone walls, dilapidated buildings, brush piles, and haystacks, the Aesculapian snake is a quite agile and fast-moving predator. It climbs tree trunks very nimbly but when forced to flee will also slither away across the ground at considerable speed. It enjoys basking in the morning sun and when warmed, it moves about its favorite haunts in search of mice and voles and other rodents. It kills its prey by constriction. The females are oviparous and lay their 5–20 eggs during the summer. They hatch after 2 months' incubation.

162 ELAPHE OBSOLETA
Rat snake

Classification Order Squamata, Family Colubridae.
Distribution Southeastern Canada, central-eastern United States, northern Mexico.
Identification The largest non-poisonous snake over much of its range, this powerfully built constrictor may be plainly colored, striped, or blotched. Its shiny scales are weakly keeled. Individuals from northern localities (subspecies *Elaphe obsoleta obsoleta*) are uniformly black with no markings. Those snakes with stripes are basically red, brownish or yellowish (as in the subspecies *E. o. quadrivittata* from southeastern United States, illustrated in the photograph), with 4 dark longitudinal bands, while those with spotted markings are greyish or brownish-yellow with large dark patches on the back. Total length: 3–8¼ ft (.9–2.5 m).
Habitat Moist hardwood forests, rocky timbered slopes, old farm fields, river swamps, everglades, wooded canyons.
Biology As its name implies, this serpent is a rodent control specialist. It is a superb climber and has little difficulty ascending to the canopy of trees or the rafters of abandoned farm buildings while foraging. Sometimes it will take up residence in a tree hollow. During spring and autumn it is active during the day but becomes more nocturnal during warm summer months. The females are oviparous, laying 5–30 eggs in the summer.

163 ELAPHE QUATUORLINEATA
Four-lined snake

Classification Order Squamata, Family Colubridae.
Distribution Southeastern Europe and southwestern Asia.
Identification Largest snake in its range. It is a robust species with lightly keeled back scales which give it a rough appearance. Young are gray or yellowish-gray with a series of large dark marks on the back or one or two lines of small, black spots on the flanks. Adults living in western areas are yellowish-brown or grayish above, with 4 dark back stripes extending from nape of the neck to tail. Eastern populations lack stripes and have markings very similar to those of the young. Total length: 2¾–8¼ ft (.8–2.5 m).
Habitat Rocky overgrown hillsides, woodland edges, streamside thickets, marshlands.
Biology In contrast to its relative, the Aesculapian snake, the four-lined snake prefers damper environments, often close to water, and heavier cover. It is especially active on warm, overcast days and during late afternoon hours. It is largely terrestrial, but can also climb trees and bushes with agility. The young feed principally on lizards and the adults relish small mammals and nestlings. The females lay their eggs in early summer. The young, when they hatch after 2 months' incubation, measure 8–12 in (20–30 cm).

---

164 ELAPHE TAENIURA
Oriental beauty snake

Classification Order Squamata, Family Colubridae.
Distribution Central-southern China, Assam, Burma, Thailand, Laos, Vietnam, Taiwan.
Identification This snake has a fairly flat head quite distinct from the trunk, large eyes with a round pupil and a dark stripe extending from the back of the eyes to the corner of the mouth. Its color is yellowish-gray or olive, with many irregularly scattered dark spots at the front of the body and a light band along the vertebral line from midbody to tail tip. On either flank, at the rear of the body and on the tail there is a row of large black blotches, close together and often fused. Total length: 5–8¾ ft (1.5–2.6 m).
Habitat Woodland edges, rocky ground with plenty of clefts and shrubs, cave entrances.
Biology This species frequents a variety of habitats and is often seen near cultivated fields and farms where it hunts rodents and birds. It is active mainly by day, spending much of its time on the ground, but when pursued or is hunting prey it will climb trees and bushes with ease. It is not aggressive by nature and normally flees rapidly at the slightest sign of danger. It is an egg layer.

165   ERPETON TENTACULATUM
Tentacled snake

Classification   Order Squamata, Family Colubridae.
Distribution   Thailand, Cambodia, Vietnam.
Identification   The species has a flat trapezoidal-shaped head, small eyes with a vertical pupil and a snout with two tentacle-like appendages. The body is fairly flat and stiff and is covered with strongly keeled scales. Its back is variable but typically is brown or reddish-brown color with two longitudinal dark stripes running down the vertebral line from nape to tail. Total length: 16–28 in (41–70 cm).
Habitat   Sluggish streams and river backwaters, swamps, brackish lagoons.
Biology   This snake lives exclusively in water. It is sedentary and anchors itself to aquatic vegetation with its prehensile tail. It is not aggressive by nature and feeds mainly on fish. The females are ovoviviparous and give birth to 6–13 young at a time. The two tentacles at the tip of the snout are not actively mobile but they may act as bait to attract prey, or they may have a sensory function, enabling the snake to locate fish in muddy water.

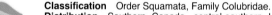

166   HETERODON NASICUS
Western snake, Western hognose snake

Classification   Order Squamata, Family Colubridae.
Distribution   Southern Canada, central-southern United States, northern Mexico.
Identification   Well named for its sharply upturned and pointed snout, the chunkily-built hognose has a large head with big eyes and a broad neck. Its scales are keeled. The back is tan, brown, or yellowish-gray, with a series of large dark spots on the back and 2–3 rows of spots on either flank. The underside is patterned with large, black blotches. Total length: 16–36 in (41–91 cm).
Habitat   Prairies, dry open woodlands, sandy-soiled floodplains, farm fields.
Biology   Neither fast-moving nor especially agile, this species is a burrowing specialist. Using its short, pointed snout, it burrows into the substrata to avoid the hot midday sun or night chill. It also ferrets out buried toads, lizards, snakes, or their eggs. Although completely harmless to humans, it is often mistaken for a rattlesnake because of its stout features and defensive habits. When disturbed, the "puff adder" spreads its neck, inflates its body, hisses, and strikes. If that fails, it may roll over and play dead. It rarely bites humans. Females lay 4–23 eggs.

167 LAMPROPELTIS GETULUS
Common kingsnake

Classification   Order Squamata, Family Colubridae.
Distribution   United States and northern Mexico.
Identification   The species has a relatively small head, hardly distinguishable from the neck, eyes with round pupils, and smooth scales. Color and pattern vary according to the location of the population. The basic color is usually brown or blackish, with numerous light spots (ssp. *holbrooki*) or wide crossbands (ssp. *californiae* and *floridana*) or narrow (ssp. *getulus* and *splendida*). Individuals of the ssp. *niger*, however, are nearly uniformly blackish. Total length: 3–6½ ft (.9–2 m).
Habitat   Coastal pinewoods, everglades, marshes, dry rocky wooded hillsides, prairies, arid scrubland, chaparral.
Biology   Except during the warmest days of summer when it moves at night, the kingsnake is active in the morning and late afternoon. It is primarily terrestrial but its varied diet may cause this agile species to take to shrubs in search of prey – snakes, lizards, small birds, and rodents. Kingsnakes are powerful constrictors and suffocate prey before swallowing it. The females are oviparous, laying their eggs during the summer. These take 2–3 months to hatch.

168 MALPOLON MONSPESSULANUS
Montpellier snake

Classification   Order Squamata, Family Colubridae.
Distribution   North Africa, Iberia, Mediterranean France, northwestern Italy, Balkan peninsula, southwestern Asia.
Identification   This snake has a long head, with a peculiar concavity between its exceptionally large "hooded" eyes. The snout overhangs the lower jaw. Coloration varies from gray to black or reddish-brown to olive, with or without dark spots and reticulations. Two lines of dark spots run along the flanks and these, in some individuals, may fuse to form parallel longitudinal stripes. Total length: 3–6½ ft (.9–2 m).
Habitat   Dry sandy or rocky scrublands, open woods, vegetated coastal dunes, old farms.
Biology   The Montpellier snake is an extremely agile, fast-moving sight hunter. It is generally terrestrial although it can climb bushes and trees quite nimbly. It holds the front part of its body off the ground while hunting to increase its field of vision. Darting lizards, snakes, and small mammals are chased down and quickly immobilized by the venom. It is not considered dangerous to man, but should not be handled carelessly. An egg-layer.

169 NATRIX NATRIX
Grass snake

Classification   Order Squamata, Family Colubridae.
Distribution   Northwest Africa, Europe, western Asia.
Identification   This keeled-scaled species has an elongated head clearly distinct from the body, and big eyes with round pupils. Color is extremely variable and may be steel-gray, olive-brown or black. Dark crossbars and spots may be present on side and back and two light body stripes are sometimes seen. Most populations have a dark-bordered white, yellow, or orange collar behind the head. In some localities the representatives lack the collar and dark markings. Total length: 2–6½ ft (.6–2 m).
Habitat   Wet meadows, marshes, banks of rivers, streams, and canals, margins of drainage ditches, ponds, lakes.
Biology   Although it is strongly associated with water in many parts of its range, it is the least aquatic of Europe's three water snakes. In the northern part of its range, it can be encountered in farmlands or open woodlands some distance from water. It is active mainly by day, feeding on frogs, toads, salamanders, and fish. It is not aggressive and seldom bites. The females are oviparous and lay their eggs in hollow logs or under haystacks, compost heaps, or manure piles.

---

170 NERODIA TAXISPILOTA
Brown water snake

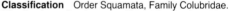
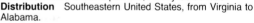

Classification   Order Squamata, Family Colubridae.
Distribution   Southeastern United States, from Virginia to Alabama.
Identification   This species has a broad, flat head, and a stocky, heavy body with keeled scales giving it a rough appearance. It is dull brown with a row of large dark quadrangular marks along the vertebral line. A similar series of marks runs along the sides of the body from nape to tail. The underside is yellowish with numerous squarish brown blotches. Total length: 28–69 in (71–175 cm).
Habitat   Rivers, large ponds and lakes, marshes and swamps.
Biology   This sun-lover likes to bask on banks or vegetation that hangs over water. It is active mainly by day, spending the early hours of the morning coiled up in the sun. After warming, it forages for frogs and fish among the emergent vegetation close to the shoreline. Agile and speedy in its movements, it is quite fierce by nature. When grabbed it emits a foul-smelling secretion from its cloaca and attempts repeatedly to bite its captor. The females are live-bearers and give birth to 14–58 young at a time.

171 THAMNOPHIS SIRTALIS
Common garter snake

Classification Order Squamata, Family Colubridae.
Distribution Canada, United States, and northern Mexico.
Identification Like its watersnake relatives, its head is slightly enlarged at the back, the snout is relatively short and the eyes are of average size with round pupils. Scales are similarly keeled. Coloration and markings are very variable. Individuals may be dark brown, black, green or olive with well-defined back and sidestripes present. Alternating black spots or reddish blotches are often seen between back and side stripes. Total length: 18–51½ in (46–131 cm).
Habitat Banks of streams, pools and lakes, wet meadows, prairie swales, damp woodlands.
Biology North America's most common and widespread species, the garter snake frequents a wide range of moist habitats across the land. It is primarily terrestrial and active day and night in warm weather. On cool days, the early morning hours are spent warming up in the sun on stones and rotting trunks. The diet is very varied, including earthworms, amphibians, fish, and small rodents. The females are ovo-viviparous and give birth to 6–50 or more young at a time.

---

172 THELOTORNIS KIRTLANDII
African twig snake

Classification Order Squamata, Family Colubridae.
Distribution Central and west Africa.
Identification The lance-shaped head with large eyes and keyhole-shaped pupils characterize this extremely slender, whip-tailed snake. Its scales are weakly keeled. The back is light green, grayish or brownish, with or without light spots and dark crossbars. A black speckled reddish band or line extends from the tip of the snout, through the eye, to the temporal region. There is a large black transverse marking on the neck. Total length: 4–6 ft (1.2–1.8 m).
Habitat Tropical rain forests.
Biology The African twig snake is strictly arboreal by habit and moves extremely fast. The cryptic coloration makes it very difficult to see in the tree foliage and its extremely keen vision enables it to locate prey from quite a distance. It feeds on lizards, catching them by ambush, but eats nestling birds and snakes as well. It is not aggressive by nature, but when threatened it inflates its neck and throat and makes lunging strikes. The strikes are a bluff and bites are very rare. Its venom is very powerful and its effects are similar to that of the boomslang. Females are egg-layers.

173 XENOCHROPIS PISCATOR
Checkered keelback snake

Classification Order Squamata, Family Colubridae.
Distribution India, southern China, Taiwan, Indochina, Malaccan peninsula, Indonesia.
Identification The head is fairly flat and hardly distinguished from the neck, and the eyes, of average size, have round pupils. The back is covered with strongly keeled, shingle-like scales and is brownish-gray or olive with quadrangular black spots arranged in rows. Two black diagonal stripes radiate from the eye to rear of the upper jaw. A V-shaped black mark on the upper part of the neck may be present. Total length: 24–48 in (61–122 cm).
Habitat Banks of rivers and swamps, rice paddies, and irrigation ditches.
Biology This snake is always found in or near wetlands with plenty of vegetation. It swims with great agility and feeds principally on fish and amphibians but occasionally kills small snakes as well. It is not aggressive but will repeatedly strike if cornered or it is picked up. The females are oviparous and lay their eggs under plant detritus on the banks of pools and swamps.

174 ACANTHOPHIS ANTARCTICUS
Death adder

Classification Order Squamata, Family Elapidae.
Distribution Northern, eastern, and southern Australia.
Identification The viper-like species has a broad, triangular head, a short stout body, and a thin tail ending in a curved soft spine. The small eyes, with vertically elliptical pupils, appear hooded. It ranges from pale gray to deep reddish-brown in color and is marked with irregular crossbands. The tail tip is usually white or cream. Total length: 16–40 in (41–101 cm).
Habitat Forest, open woodlands, semiarid scrublands.
Biology During the day the death adder stays hidden under decaying leaves, or half-buried in the soil, often close to trees and bushes. At dusk it emerges from its lair to hunt for lizards, small rodents, and birds. From an ambush position it will lure their prey within striking distance by twitching the tip of its distinctive tail. Their venom is extremely toxic to prey and also highly dangerous for humans. They are considered one of the world's deadliest snakes. They produce up to 20 young in a litter.

175 BUNGARUS FASCIATUS
Banded krait

Classification   Order Squamata, Family Elapidae.
Distribution   Northeastern India, Indochina, Malay peninsula and Archipelago.
Identification   This snake has a flat head hardly distinguishable from the neck and small eyes with round pupils. Scales are smooth and glossy. Wide black and yellow bands encircle the body. There is almost always an inverted V-shaped mark on the top of the head. Total length: 4–7 ft (1.2–2.1 m).
Habitat   Open terrain with plenty of grass and bushes, cultivated lands, forest margins and clearings.
Biology   The banded krait is found in grassy fields and meadows close to pools and streams. It is active mainly at night and normally spends the day hidden under stones or fallen trunks. It feeds on snakes and lizards. Although it has a highly toxic venom, it is far from aggressive and does not as a rule bite humans even when molested. The females are oviparous and, having laid their 6–10 eggs, often remain coiled about them until they hatch.

---

176 DENDROASPIS POLYLEPIS
Black mamba

Classification   Order Squamata, Family Elapidae.
Distribution   Eastern and central-southern Africa.
Identification   The head is long and narrow, the eyes large with round pupils, and the fairly slender body covered with smooth, glossy scales. Adults are uniformly gun-metal to olive-brown or yellowish-brown, while the underparts are grayish-white tinged with yellow or green. The lining of the mouth is blue-black. Total length: 6½–14 ft (2–4.3 m).
Habitat   Savannas, semiarid bush country, open woodlands, rocky outcrops.
Biology   The black mamba is the largest venomous snake in Africa. It is the most terrestrial of the mambas, and is active mainly by day. Extremely agile and speedy, it pursues birds and small mammals and they may be repeatedly bitten. The snake waits until the injected venom has killed its victim before it begins its meal. A termite mound, tree hollow, or rock crevice may serve as home. If surprised and cornered, it is highly aggressive and rears the front of its body, flattens its neck, and gapes its mouth. They do not bluff, heed this warning! Their neurotoxic and cardiotoxic venom is extremely potent. Females often lay their dozen eggs in a termite nest.

177 LATICAUDA COLUBRINA
Yellow-lipped sea brait

Classification Order Squamata, Family Hydrophiidae.
Distribution Tropical coasts of the eastern Indian Ocean and western Pacific.
Identification This species has a large, blunt, cobra-like head, not distinct from the neck, with nostrils positioned at the sides of the snout. The body is cylindrical and covered with smooth, overlapping scales, while the tail is somewhat laterally compressed. The body is bluish-gray with numerous large black rings which extend around the belly. The snout and upper lips are yellow, while the rest of the head is blackish. Total length: 24–55 in (61–140 cm).
Habitat Coastal waters, brackish lagoons, atolls, mangrove swamps.
Biology Unlike other sea snakes, the sea braits spend long periods of time on land where they come to bask after dining on eels in nearby waters. It moves with considerable ease both in water and on dry land, and is active mainly at night. During the day it hides in rocky or coral crevices or vegetative debris but often exposes parts of its body to the sun's warming rays. It is not aggressive by temperament and although its venom is potentially lethal, it does not attempt to bite even when roughly handled. While other sea snakes are live-bearers, sea brait females lay eggs. About 4–6 eggs are laid under palm fronds or in a rotting log.

---

178 MICRURUS FULVIUS
Eastern coral snake

Classification Order Squamata, Family Elapidae.
Distribution Southeastern United States and northeastern Mexico.
Identification This tri-coloured species has a small rounded head that is hardly distinguishable from the neck, and a cylindrical body covered with smooth, glossy scales. The body is encircled with broad alternating black and red rings separated by narrower bright yellow rings. The snout is completely black, while the top of the head is adorned with a transverse yellow band. Total length: 22–47½ in (56–121 cm).
Habitat Pinewoods, hardwood hammocks, banks of streams and pools, and woodland edge in the East; cedar brakes and rocky hillsides, the West.
Biology Secretive by nature, the coral snake is not often seen and it is often more common in an area than people believe. It is most active on the surface in spring and autumn and moves about in the early morning and late afternoon. It feeds on lizards and small snakes. Coral snake envenomation is serious and can be life threatening. While small specimens have some difficulty biting, larger specimens have respectable fangs which can quickly deliver a dangerous dose of venom. Don't handle! An egg-layer.

179 NAJA NAJA
Asiatic cobra

Classification   Order Squamata, Family Elapidae.
Distribution   Turkestan, Pakistan, India, Sri Lanka, southern China, Indochina, Malaccan peninsula, Malay Archipelago, Philippines.
Identification   When disturbed, this snake spreads its neck laterally to form a distinct hood. It has a large, flattened head, covered by broad, symmetrical plates, and smooth scales on its body. The color of the backside is extremely variable and may be brown, yellowish, olive-gray or black, with or without light or dark crossbars and spots. On the neck there is frequently a characteristic black and white pattern that may resemble a pair of spectacles or a bullseye, but sometimes this mark is completely absent. Total length: 4–7½ ft (1.2–2.3 m).
Habitat   Forest margins and clearings, to rice fields and suburbia.
Biology   The Asiatic cobra is active mainly at dusk and during the night but it may be seen basking during the day. It feeds primarily on rodents, but birds, lizards, and toads are also eaten. It is rather excitable and when confronted by an aggressor rears up the front of its body, "hoods," and stands its ground. It is the favorite of snake charmers. Its venom is highly neurotoxic and accounts for the death of many thousands of humans annually. One to several dozen eggs are laid in an abandoned termite mound or warm, moist, protected environment.

180 OPHIOPHAGUS HANNAH
King cobra

Classification   Order Squamata, Family Elapidae.
Distribution   India, southern China, Indochina, Malaccan peninsula, Malay Archipelago, Philippines.
Identification   This species has a broad, flattened head covered by large, symmetrical plates. Smooth scales cover the body which is tan, olive-brown or black, with or without numerous light crossbands. These bands are clearly visible in the young but often disappear entirely in adults. The belly is cream or yellowish, with various dark markings. Total length: 8–18 ft (2.4–5.5 m).
Habitat   Forest margins and clearings, bamboo thickets, overgrown fields.
Biology   The king cobra or "hamadryad" is the largest living venomous snake. Very agile and fast-moving, it is active almost only by day. It feeds principally on other snakes. It is a sight hunter and a good climber and will follow prey into trees without hesitation. Despite its size, it is not particularly aggressive, and usually retreats when disturbed. If pressured, it will "hood" and strike. While human bites are rare, the venom of this cobra is extremely toxic and if envenomation occurs death will follow if aggressive antivenom isn't started quickly. Females construct a two-chambered nest of leaf-litter. The lower one holds the eggs, the upper the guarding female.

181 AGKISTRODON CONTORTRIX
Copperhead

Classification Order Squamata, Family Viperidae.
Distribution Eastern United States from Massachusetts to west Texas.
Identification The head is broad and flat, clearly distinct from the neck, the snout is slightly upturned, the eyes are relatively small with vertical pupils, and a large pit is present between the eye and nostrils. The body is fairly stout and covered with weakly keeled scales. It is copper, orangish, or pinkish in color with a number of chestnut or reddish-brown crossbands which are pinched at the back's midline. The top of the head is completely unmarked. Total length: 22–53 in (56–135 cm).
Habitat Rocky wooded hillsides, wooded areas near water, vicinity of canyon springs and streams.
Biology The copperhead frequents leaf litter and wood piles, old stone walls, and construction litter dumped at the edge of moist woodlands or near water. In spring and autumn they are diurnally active but become nocturnal during warm summer months. It feeds on small rodents, lizards and frogs, killing its prey with venom injected with its two enlarged fangs. Bites are painful but not considered very dangerous to man. Copperheads bear living young, about 6–10 in number, in the autumn.

182 BITIS ARIETANS
Puff adder

Classification Order Squamata, Family Viperidae.
Distribution Africa.
Identification This massive, bloated looking viper has a large triangular head with small eyes with vertical pupils and nostrils positioned at the top of the snout. The bulky body is thick and heavy and ends with an extremely short and thin tail. Coloration is rather variable but basically shades of brown with a series of light or dark V-shaped crossbands. Each side of the head displays two dark oblique bands, situated respectively below and behind the eye. Total length: 2¼–6 ft (.7–1.8 m).
Habitat Savannas, semiarid grasslands, woodlands, scrublands.
Biology The puff adder is Africa's most widely distributed snake and, with the exception of high mountain tops, arid deserts, and rainforest interior, can be expected anywhere. It is somewhat slow and lazy in its movements and is active principally at twilight and during the night when it ambushes rodents, ground birds, and toads. The females are ovo-viviparous and give birth to 20–80 or more young at a time. The snake has a fairly toxic venom and bites are very serious. Luckily, bites are very rare.

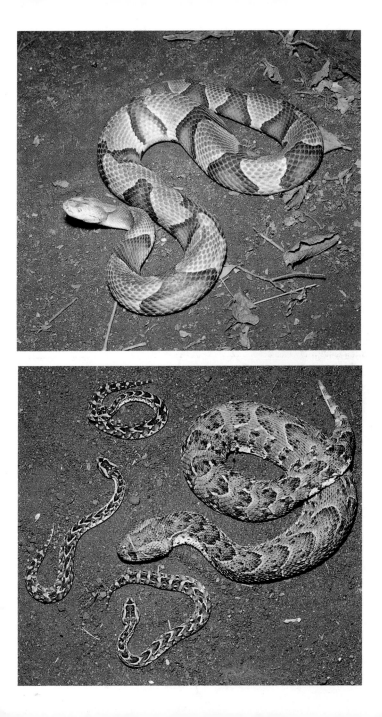

183 BOTHROPS SCHLEGELI
Eyelash viper

Classification Order Squamata, Family Viperidae.
Distribution Southern Mexico to Ecuador and Venezuela.
Identification The species has a broad, flat, triangular head, small eyes with vertical pupils and straight, pointed scales above the eyes. Scales are keeled. Coloration is exceptionally variable: some are lichen-green with pink blotches, others orangish, salmon pink, or tan with contrasting crossbands or reticulations, and some individuals are brilliant golden-yellow, with a scattering of dark flecks. Total length: 16–24 in (41–61 cm).
Habitat Tropical rain forests.
Biology This prehensile-tailed, arboreal snake is the most commonly encountered "palm viper" in its range. It is common along forest streams, brushy edge habitat, and plantations where frog and lizard prey are plentiful. They are not particularly aggressive but do not hesitate to strike if teased. Bites are painful but rarely life threatening. Females are live-bearers, giving birth to about 6–12 young annually.

184 CALLOSELASMA RHODOSTOMA
Malayan pit viper

Classification Order Squamata, Family Viperidae.
Distribution Indochina, Malaccan peninsula, Java and Sumatra.
Identification The head is triangular with large scales on its crown and the small eyes have vertical pupils. The snout is pointed and slightly upturned. The fairly sturdy body has smooth dorsal scales. The back is reddish-brown with a series of dark brown crossbands which narrow along the back's midline. A light longitudinal stripe extends from eye to nape of neck. There is a wide light-colored band on the lip scales. Total length: 24–40 in (61–102 cm).
Habitat Forest margins and clearings, plantations.
Biology This species is mainly encountered in forested areas where it normally spends the day coiled up under stones or hidden in dense vegetation. At twilight it leaves its shelter to hunt for food, consisting of small mammals, birds, and frogs. It is fairly aggressive by nature and when molested assumes a characteristic threat posture, curling up its body and vibrating the tip of its tail. Females lay 12–25 eggs which they guard until hatching 6 or 7 weeks later.

185 CAUSUS RHOMBEATUS
Rhombic night adder

Classification Order Squamata, Family Viperidae.
Distribution Central Africa (excluding Saharan regions), eastern and southern Africa.
Identification The head is covered with large symmetrical plates like colubrids. Pupils are round and body scales are weakly keeled. The back is olive-gray to pinkish-brown, with a series of pale-edged rhombic blotches along the vertebral line. There is invariably a dark V-shaped mark on the head. Total length: 16–40 in (41–102 cm).
Habitat Moist savannas and grasslands.
Biology Nocturnally active as its name implies, it spends the day in a termite mound or hiding under rocks or logs. As a rule it is slow-moving but when attacked becomes alert and aggressive, assuming a characteristic threat posture in which it inflates its body, flattens its neck and huffs and hisses. It feeds on toads and small rodents. It lays 15–26 eggs in summer which take two months to hatch. There are no recorded human fatalities from night adder bites.

---

186 CERASTES CERASTES
Desert horned viper

Classification Order Squamata, Family Viperidae.
Distribution North Africa and southwestern Asia.
Identification This snake has a very broad, flat, triangular head, and small eyes with vertical pupils. A large, ribbed, horn-like scale is usually present above the eyes. The body is thickset and covered with heavily keeled scales; the tail short and slender. Pale brown, brownish-yellow or gray in color, its back is marked with large, dark spots which are often fused to form crossbars. Total length: 18–30 in (46–76 cm).
Habitat Sandy deserts with rock outcrops.
Biology The horned viper is adapted to a nocturnal existence in a very harsh and arid environment. It spends the day inside lairs where the temperature and humidity are more or less constant. When alarmed or attacked by a predator it buries itself or rubs loops of its body together to make a rasping noise like the saw-scaled viper. It moves by sidewinding. Its diet is mainly lizards and small rodents. These are ambushed and immobilized with a powerful venom. Horned vipers are egg-layers.

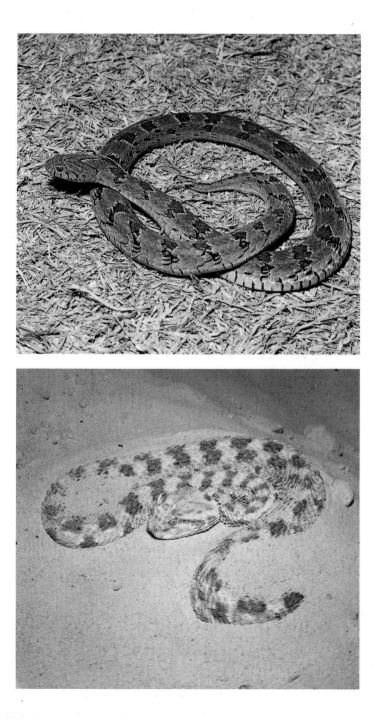

187 CROTALUS ADAMANTEUS
Eastern diamondback rattlesnake

Classification   Order Squamata, Family Viperidae.
Distribution   Southeastern United States; coastal plain from North Carolina to Mississippi.
Identification   The species has an exceptionally large head, small eyes with vertical pupils and prominent scutes over the brows. The body is very stout and covered with keeled scales. The tail is rather short, banded with dark rings, and ends in a well-developed rattle. A series of large, dark brown, diamond-shaped blotches outlined in thin bands of black and cream, mark the midline of the back. Prominent diagonal light stripes are on the side of the head. Total length: 3–8 ft (.9–2.4 m).
Habitat   Pinewoods, edges of wet savannas, lowland woods of evergreen oaks.
Biology   The Eastern diamondback rattlesnake is the largest and most dangerous venomous snake in the United States. In the spring and autumn it emerges from a stump hole or gopher tortoise burrow in the morning and late afternoon, whereas in summer it becomes more nocturnal. From an ambush point, it will patiently wait for a rabbit, squirrel, or other rodent to pass within striking distance. Its heat-recepting pits help guide its strike. The deadly venom works quickly and the diamondback unerringly tracks the bitten prey. Food is eaten head first. Between 7–21 young are born in late summer.

188 ECHIS CARINATUS
Saw-scaled viper

Classification   Order Squamata, Family Viperidae.
Distribution   Africa north of the equator and southern Asia (to India and Sri Lanka).
Identification   The head is broad and flat, the snout is short and the moderately-sized eyes have vertical pupils and yellow irises. The upper surfaces of the head, trunk and tail are covered with small, strongly keeled scales. The back may be brown, grayish, brownish-yellow, or reddish with a series of light spots, sometimes fused to form transverse bands, along the vertebral line. There is a row of light marks, sometimes merging to form a kind of wavy stripe, on either flank. Total length: 15–32 in (38–81 cm).
Habitat   Deserts, semiarid scrub forest.
Biology   The saw-scaled viper is active by night, feeding principally on small rodents and lizards. It is agile and fast-moving across sandy substrates with a peculiar form of locomotion known as sidewinding. It possesses a highly potent, haemotoxic venom and is probably one of the most dangerous and feared members of the viper family. Writhing coils of startled snakes produce a loud rasping sound. This activity may be followed by vicious leaping strikes.

189 SISTRURUS CATENATUS
Massasauga

Classification   Order Squamata, Family Viperidae.
Distribution   North America, from Ontario to southeastern Arizona and northeastern Mexico.
Identification   This pigmy rattler has 9 enlarged scales on top of its flat head. Its stout body has keeled scales. The short stocky tail ends in a well-developed rattle. The back is gray or brownish-gray, with a series of large, dark, rounded spots along the vertebral line and a row of smaller spots on either flank. There is a brown band on each side of the head, extending from the eye to the rear of the jaw. Total length: 18–39½ in (46–100 cm).
Habitat   Bogs, marshlands, and floodplains in the east; wet and dry prairies to rocky hillsides, the west.
Biology   The ''swamp rattler'' has an unusual geographic distribution. Habitats vary considerably but wet prairies and river bottoms and adjacent open fields appear to be preferred. Unlike many snakes, they do not hibernate communally in an upland den. Instead they overwinter singly in a mammal or crayfish burrow. Spring rains and rising water stimulate them to emerge. They primarily eat small rodents. Although it has fairly potent venom, it is not an aggressive snake and normally bites only when molested. The females give birth to 2–20 young at a time.

190 TRIMERESURUS STEJNEGERI
Chinese green tree viper

Classification   Order Squamata, Family Viperidae.
Distribution   Central and southeastern China, islands of Hainan and Taiwan.
Identification   The head is broad, flat and triangular, covered with small keeled scales. The eyes are large with a vertical pupil. The back is uniformly dark green, the lower side of each flank displays a longitudinal cream stripe. In some males this stripe is often bordered by a thin reddish band. The end of the tail is normally reddish-brown. Total length: 16–30 in (41–76 cm).
Habitat   Moist woodland edges, bamboo thickets, brushy streamsides.
Biology   This snake is arboreal by habit, with a prehensile tail that enables it to cling tightly to branches. It is nocturnally active and feeds principally on frogs and small mammals. Luckily this common viper is not aggressive by nature and its haemotoxic venom does not cause serious medical emergencies for bite victims. This pit viper bears living young.

191 VIPERA AMMODYTES
Long-nosed viper

Classification Order Squamata, Family Viperidae.
Distribution Southeastern Europe and southwestern Asia.
Identification The long-nosed viper has a flat triangular head, eyes with a vertical pupil and a snout with a small upward-pointing "horn", covered with small scales. The body is quite stout, with strongly keeled back scales, and the tail relatively short. It is gray or brownish-gray, with a thick black zig-zag extending down the midline of the entire body. To either side of the backstripe is a longitudinal row of poorly defined spots. Total length: 22–37 in (56–94 cm).
Habitat Dry rocky slopes and hills with scattered shrubs, stone walls near cultivated fields, woodland edge.
Biology This snake frequents sunny areas and enjoys basking in a prominent spot among rocks, on a stone wall, or branches of shrubs. Although it is active in the morning and late afternoon, it spends the hottest part of the day in a retreat. During warm weather it hunts at night. It feeds principally on small mammals and lizards. Copulation, preceded by male combat, occurs in spring. The females are ovoviviparous and give birth to about 6–12 young in late summer.

192 VIPERA ASPIS
Asp viper

Classification Order Squamata, Family Viperidae.
Distribution Northeastern Spain, France, southwestern Germany, Switzerland, Italy, Elba and Sicily.
Identification This viper has a broad triangular head, eyes with vertical pupils and a snout that is slightly curved upward. Dorsal color is very variable and may be gray, brown, reddish-brown or black. As a rule the middle of the back displays a series of dark squarish blotches or crossbars that either alternate or are fused to form a vertebral stripe. Occasionally a zig-zag pattern is seen. All black individuals are known. Total length: 20–33 in (51–84 cm).
Habitat Woodland edges and clearings, sunny scrublands, hilly and low mountain terrain, rocky ground with sparse vegetation.
Biology The asp viper is somewhat sensitive to daily temperature extremes and limits its activities to morning and late afternoon periods. In warm muggy weather it often becomes active at night. Food consists mainly of voles, mice, shrews, and lizards. The females are ovoviviparous and give birth to 4–18 young at a time.

193 VIPERA BERUS
Adder

Classification   Order Squamata, Family Viperidae.
Distribution   Northern and central-eastern Europe, central and northern Asia.
Identification   The flat head is covered on top by three large plates, the snout is flattened and not upturned and the relatively small eyes have vertical pupils. The dorsal color is rather variable, either gray, brownish or reddish. There is a dark band or zig-zag stripe along the vertebral line which extends from the nape to the tip of the tail. On the rear of the head are two dark converging stripes, sometimes joined to form an X or inverted V. Total length: 20–35 in (50–89 cm).
Habitat   Woodland margins and clearings, rocky brushy hillsides, moors, coastal dunes, river banks.
Biology   The adder or common viper spends the winter hibernating inside underground burrows dug by rodents or under roots and tree stumps, and normally leads an active life from April to September. Its diet is quite varied and includes small mammals, amphibians, nestlings, and lizards. Young, 3–20 in number, are born in late summer. Females in the northernmost areas do not reproduce annually. Influenced by climate, altitude, and the annual abundance of food, reproduction may only occur every two or three years.

194 VIPERA RUSSELLI
Russell's viper

Classification   Order Squamata, Family Viperidae.
Distribution   Pakistan, India, Sri Lanka, southern China, Taiwan, Indochina, Indonesia.
Identification   This species has a wide head covered with small overlapping keeled scales, a square snout with big nostrils and eyes with vertical pupils. The body is stout and heavy while the tail is short and slender. Backside color is pale brown with a longitudinal row of large oval black-ringed spots along the vertebral line. A series of similar spots runs along each flank from the nape to the tip of the tail. Total length: 3–5½ ft (.9–1.7 m).
Habitat   Margins of woods and forests, brushy fields, mountain meadows, cultivated lands, thickets near villages.
Biology   Russell's viper is active mainly at twilight and during the night, remaining coiled up under stones and bushes by day. It feeds on small rodents which it strikes from ambush. Prey is very quickly killed by its potent venom. As a rule it is rather slow and lazy but when irritated becomes quite aggressive, hisses loudly and strikes out with great force and speed. This viper is a leading cause of snake bite accidents. Untreated bites have a high mortality rate. Females are very prolific, giving birth to 1–5 dozen young.

195 BLANUS CINEREUS
European worm lizard

Classification Order Squamata, Family Amphisbaenidae.
Distribution Algeria, Morocco, and Iberian peninsula.
Identification This reptile has a wormlike appearance and possesses no legs. The head is small and triangular, hardly distinct from the trunk, and the extremely tiny eyes are positioned beneath transparent scales. Both the body and the short tail have a series of grooves which separate rings of small square plates. A prominent longitudinal groove runs down the vertebral line and either flank. The upper surfaces are a fairly uniform gray, light brown or chestnut and tinged with pink or violet. Total length: 6–11 in (15–28 cm).
Habitat Moist sandy or humus rich soils, farmlands, pinewoods.
Biology The worm lizard lives almost exclusively underground and only occasionally comes to the surface in heavy rain or damp nights. It frequents loose soils and uses its snout to dig long tunnels, inside which it can move easily backward and forward. It feeds on earthworms and various arthropods, locating its prey by smell and touch. Sexually mature individuals mate in the spring. The females are oviparous and lay a single large egg.

196 TROGONOPHIS WIEGMANNI
Wiegmann's burrowing lizard

Classification Order Squamata, Family Trogonophidae.
Distribution Northwest Africa.
Identification This species has a fairly small head, not distinct from the neck, and tiny eyes positioned beneath small transparent scales. There are no limbs and the body, cylindrical and elongated, is covered with tiny rectangular scales arranged in regular rings. These scales are alternately light and dark, so that the overall appearance of the reptile is that of a densely designed chessboard. The tail is extremely short and conical in form. Total length: 6–9½ in (15–24 cm).
Habitat Sandy and loamy soil regions.
Biology This species has burrowing habits, spending most of the day excavating long tunnels, inside which it can move as quickly backward as forward, and only occasionally venturing to the surface. It feeds almost exclusively on ants and termites, often hunting its prey under stones. The females are ovoviviparous and give birth in late summer to 2–5 fairly large offspring.

197 SPHENODON PUNCTATUS
Tuatara

Classification Order Rhynchocephalia, Family Sphenodontidae.
Distribution Small New Zealand islands in the Cook Strait, the Gulf of Hauraki and the Bay of Plenty.
Identification This "living fossil" has a huge head, eyes with vertical pupils and nictitating membranes, a medium-sized laterally compressed tail, and stout limbs with five claws on both hands and feet. A crest of horny tubercles runs down the vertebral line of the body and extends from head to tail. Unlike other living Lepidosauria, the tuatara has a snout with a tip that curves slightly downward to form a kind of beak, and a skull which retains its typical diapsid structure. It is light brown or gray in color, with a dense sprinkling of yellow spots. Total length: 14–24 in (36–61 cm).
Habitat Cliff bound rocky islands with plenty of low forest or scrub cover.
Biology Rhynchocephalians have been in existence for more than 200 million years and the tuatara, the oldest sole living representative, has changed little in 60 million years. It is active at twilight and functions best when its body temperature fluctuates between 52° F (11° C) and 55° F (13° C). It feeds mainly on insects and spends the day inside underground burrows. In October and November the females lay 8–15 eggs in holes dug in the ground. The eggs hatch after 13–14 months' incubation.

198 ALLIGATOR MISSISSIPPIENSIS
American alligator

Classification Order Crocodylia, Family Alligatoridae.
Distribution Southeastern United States, from North Carolina to Texas.
Identification This large alligator has a relatively broad, flat head and a snout that is rounded at the tip. The fourth tooth of the lower jaw is enlarged but not visible when the mouth is closed, being lodged in a socket in the upper jaw. On the head, the back and the tail are longitudinal, transverse series of keeled bony plates that form a strong armor. The limbs are short and sturdy, and the feet are webbed and have sharp claws. Generally gray or black in color. Younger specimens are accented with cream or yellowish crossbands. Total length: 6½–15 ft (2–4.6 m).
Habitat Extensive swampy areas, ponds, lakes and sluggish rivers, freshwater and brackish marshes.
Biology The alligator spends much of the day basking on shores or banks of rivers and lakes, often hidden in the vegetation. They may forage actively during the day or at night. Prey includes fish, turtles, snakes, mammals, and birds. Young take insects, frogs, and small fish. The female lays her 20–60 eggs in an enormous mound nest of mud, humus, and rotting vegetation positioned in a protected area near the water's edge. After the eggs hatch the mother may stay with her young for 1–3 years.

199 CAIMAN CROCODILUS
Spectacled caiman

Classification   Order Crocodylia, Family Alligatoridae.
Distribution   Central and South America, from Mexico to Uruguay. Introduced to southern Florida.
Identification   This species has a broad, rounded snout and a characteristic bony ridge between the eyes which resembles the frame of a pair of spectacles. Both the upper and lower parts of the body are covered with an armor of dermal scutes. The sturdy tail is compressed laterally and the digits of the feet are webbed and possess sharp claws. Color is light brown or yellowish tan to olive-gray with a series of distinct or indistinct dark crossbars on body and tail. Total length: 3½–8½ ft (1–2.6 m).
Habitat   Swamps, rivers, canals, ponds.
Biology   Caimans, like the majority of crocodilians, are heavily exploited for their hides. Millions are killed annually for the exotic leather trade. They are known for their aggressive behavior and even small females will give a good account of themselves when their nest or young is being threatened. Caimans grow quickly and mature in about 5 years – about half the time required for large crocodilian species. They feed on crustaceans, molluscs, insects, fish, and amphibians.

200 CROCODYLUS NILOTICUS
Nile crocodile

Classification   Order Crocodylia, Family Crocodylidae.
Distribution   Tropical and subtropical regions of Africa, Madagascar.
Identification   This crocodile has a large head and a long, fairly narrow snout. The fourth tooth of the lower jaw fits into an external groove in the upper jaw and is therefore visible even when the mouth is closed. The neck, trunk and tail are covered on top by a solid armor of keeled, bony plates. The tail is extremely long and laterally compressed. The hind feet are webbed. Adults are olive or gray, uniformly colored or with remnants of the irregular black markings on back and sides that are seen in the young. Belly cream or yellow. Total length: 8–20 ft (2.4–6 m).
Habitat   Rivers, lakes, swamps, canals.
Biology   The Nile crocodile is a fierce and dominant carnivore. While it is usually seen basking motionless on sandbanks, this species is a very adept hunter, taking prey by ambush, pursuit, or using the tail to direct animals towards its mouth. Fish, turtles, aquatic birds, and small mammals are taken. Bigger individuals often lurk near drinking holes and may kill and drag under water large prey such as domestic goats and gazelles. Man is considered fair game.

201 CROCODYLUS POROSUS
Saltwater crocodile

Classification Order Crocodylia, Family Crocodylidae.
Distribution Southeast Asia, Indonesia, Philippines, New Guinea, and northern Australia.
Identification This species has a large head with four large dermal scutes on the nape, and a fairly long snout with a straight bony projection in front of the eyes. The keeled bony plates that form the back and tail armor are distinctly separated from the neck scutes. The hind feet are webbed. Hatchlings and young adults are yellow with numerous large dark spots on the body and tail. Older individuals become dark olive. The belly is white. Total length: 9–20 ft (2.7–6 m).
Habitat River mouths, brackish lakes, sea inlets.
Biology Perhaps the largest of the crocodylians, this gigantic reptile normally lives in estuaries and shallow coastal waters, especially near mangrove swamps. It often ventures into the open sea and some individuals may be encountered at quite a distance from shore. The diet is extremely varied and is composed of fish, crustaceans, birds, and mammals. Like the Nile crocodile, it sometimes kills domestic mammals and drags them under the surface when the latter come to drink in lakes and rivers. It is dangerous to man. Young reach sexual maturity in 10–15 years. Like other crocodilians, they are very attentive parents. Nests are guarded and hatchlings protected for protracted periods of time.

202 GAVIALIS GANGETICUS
Gharial

Classification Order Crocodylia, Family Gavialidae.
Distribution Pakistan, northern India, Nepal, Bangladesh.
Identification Its snout is extremely long and narrow with parallel sides. Color is olive with dark crossbanding. Old adults may appear uniformly gray. Sexually mature males have a characteristic swelling on the tip of the snout, in the center of which are the nostrils, its shape like that of a *ghara* (Hindu earthenware pot). According to some authors, this resemblance is the origin of the name *Gharial*, the Indian common name of the species. Total length: 13–20 ft (4–6 m).
Habitat Rivers, swampy estuaries.
Biology Known since ancient times, the gharial is the only living species of the family Gavialidae. It is highly aquatic and well adapted for life in the deep waters of great rivers. It feeds mainly on fish, catching them with the long teeth of its narrow jaws. It very seldom attacks man. Although fond of basking, they do not venture far from the water and prefer the security of mud-river sandbars. The females leave the water in the egg-laying season when they climb the sandy river banks to deposit their eggs in holes dug with their feet.

GLOSSARY

Acrodontism Type of dentition in the tuatara and lizards in which the teeth are fixed to the alveolar margin of the jaws.

Albinism Hereditary anomaly, due to a recessive autosomal gene, which consists essentially of a lack of melanistic pigments. In individuals affected by this condition, the skin and appendages are white and the pupil of the eye is red.

Amphicoelous Of vertebrae, with both the anterior and posterior surfaces of the centrum concave.

Aposematic Adjective used to describe the structures, colors, odors, behavior or special abilities which warn predators that the animal concerned has a special means of defense.

Autotomy More or less voluntary detachment of a part of the body (for example, the tail) in reaction to an external stimulus.

Burrower Animal characterized by particular morphological adaptations for digging in the ground, where it spends the greater part of its life.

Carina Keel.

Choana The internal openings of the nasal passage in the roof of the mouth.

Cloaca Common chamber into which the intestinal, urinary, and reproductive ducts empty their contents, opening to the outside through the anus.

Crest An elevated, prominent ridge or fold of flesh or bone.

Diapause State of inactivity which, in some animals, interrupts two periods of active life.

Dichromism Phenomenon whereby the male and female of the same species have different coloration.

Encephalon Synonym for the vertebrate brain. Part of the central nervous system, in front of the spinal medulla, with five recognizable regions: telencephalon, diencephalon, mesencephalon, metencephalon, and myencephalon.

Flipper Limb transformed into a kind of paddle and used for swimming (as in the marine turtles).

Gill arch Bony or cartilaginous structure in the pharyngual region of fishes and larval amphibians which supports their gills.

Gills Respiratory organs of aquatic organisms (and of some land organisms). They are formed by outgrowths of the integument or the digestive apparatus and have a fairly thin wall which permits gaseous exchanges between the animal and its aquatic environment.

Hemipenis Either one of the copulatory organs found in the base of the tail of lizards and snakes.

Hybridogenesis Reproductive mechanism which enables individuals born from the crossing of two species (hybrids) to survive indefinitely in a mixed population consisting of individuals that belong to each of the two parental species and the hybrids themselves.

Hypogean Adjective denoting an organism which habitually lives underground.

Imbricate Overlapping like roof shingles (e.g. condition in reptiles where posterior end of a given scale overlaps the anterior ends of those which follow).

Incubation Period that follows the laying of an egg, during which the embryo completes its development.

Larva Post-embryonic developmental stage (e.g. tadpole), in which the immature individual displays morphological and physiological characteristics that differ from those of the adult.

Melanism Hereditary phenomenon causing the appearance, in a population or a taxon, of individuals characterized by a uniformly black or blackish coloration.

Metamorphosis Series of morphological and physiological transformations which lead from the larval to the adult state.

Mimetism Phenomenon whereby certain organisms are able to assume the appearance of a particular object or of another organism.

Neoteny Term used to indicate the reproductive capacity of amphibians which still possess larval characteristics.

Oviduct Tubule that allows the passage of eggs from the ovary to the cloaca.

Oviparous Adjective describing an animal which lays eggs.

Ovoviviparous Adjective refering to "live-bearing" reptiles in which females retain their membranous eggs inside their bodies until hatching.

Parotid gland Subcutaneous venom-bearing gland in snakes located behind and below the eye and derived from the modification of a part of the upper labial gland.

Parotoid gland Rounded or elliptical cutaneous gland situated behind the eye of many anuran and caudate amphibians.

Parthenogenesis Reproductive mechanism whereby the egg develops without being fertilized.

Pentadactylous Adjective describing a limb with five digits.

Phenology Study of the relationship of seasonal climatic patterns and periodic biological phenomena (e.g. spring rains and salamander migrations).

Placenta Structure which enables the embryo to receive food and oxygen from the mother's body and to eliminate the products of cellular metabolism.

Polymorphism Morphological, chromatic or genetic variability which characterizes individuals making up a population or given taxon.

Prehensile Adjective which refers to an organ suitable for gripping (for example, the hand of a primate, the tail of some lizards and snakes, etc.).

Procoelous Of a vertebra, uniformly concave in front and convex in the rear.

Rattle Characteristic tail tip appendage of rattlesnakes, made up of flattened, dry horny interlocking segments that produce a buzzing sound when vibrated.

Sexual dimorphism Phenomenon whereby, in a particular species, one sex displays morphological or chromatic features different from those of the other.

Stripe Colored line that extends along any part of an animal's body surface.

Taxon Any category (subspecies, species, genus, family, class, order, etc.) of biological systematics.

Territorial Pattern of behavior in defense of a defined area, adopted by an individual or a group of individuals, against members of the same species.

Tetrapod Vertebrate provided with two paired appendages or limbs.

Thermoregulation Maintenance of body temperature at a more or less constant level thanks to special physiological or behavioral mechanisms.

Troglodyte Terrestrial or aquatic organism that lives exclusively in a cave and exhibits a series of adaptations to life underground.

Vitellus Storage material (e.g. yolk) contained in the egg and necessary for embryonic development.

Viviparous Adjective describing an animal which gives birth to young that are more or less similar to adults, already capable of surviving alone or the object of parental care. The entire embryonic development is completed inside the mother's body and food for the embryo is supplied directly by the mother through placental connections or analogous formations.

BIBLIOGRAPHY

The choice of books on amphibians and reptiles is vast. We give here a selection of some of the principal works on these two classes of vertebrates. Readers wishing to extend further their knowledge of the biology of amphibians and reptiles should consult the bibliographies included in the titles cited below.

General works
Bellairs, A. *The Life of Reptiles*, vols 1–2, Weidenfeld and Nicolson, London 1969

Duellman, W. E., and Trueb, L., *Biology of Amphibians*, McGraw-Hill Book Company, New York 1985

Ferguson, M. W. J. (ed.), *The Structure, Development and Evolution of Reptiles*, Academic Press, London 1984

Frost, D. (ed.), *Amphibian Species of the World*, Association of Systematics Collections and Allen Press, Lawrence 1984

Gans, C. (ed.), (ongoing), *Biology of the Reptilia*, Academic Press, London 1969

Goin, C. J., Goin, O. B., and Zug, G. R, *Introduction to Herpetology*, W. H. Freeman & Co., San Francisco 1978

Halliday, T., and Adler, K., *The Encyclopaedia of Reptiles and Amphibians*, G. Allen & Unwin, London 1986

Lanza, B. (ed.), *Dizionario del Regno Animale*, A. Mondadori Editore, Milan 1982

Peters, J. A., *Dictionary of Herpetology*, Hafner Publ. Co., New York and London 1964

Porter, K. R., *Herpetology*, W. B. Saunders Co., London and Toronto 1972

Webb, J. E., Wallwork, J. A., and Elgood, J. H., *Guide to Living Reptiles*, The MacMillan Press Ltd, London and Basingstoke 1978

Works on various groups of amphibians and reptiles
Bustard, R., *Sea Turtles. Their Natural History and Conservation*, Collins, London and Sydney 1972

Groombridge, B., *The IUCN Amphibia-Reptilia Red Data Book. 1. Testudines Crocodylia Rhynchocephalia*, IUCN, Gland 1982

Honegger, R. E., *Red Data Book, vol 3: Amphibia and Reptilia*, IUCN, Morges 1979

Mattison, C., *Snakes of the World*, Blandford Press, Poole 1986

Mattison, C., *Frogs and Toads of the World*, Facts on File Publ., New York 1987

Parker, H. W., and Grandison, A. G. C., *Snakes—A Natural History*, British Museum (Natural History) & Cornell University Press, Ithaca and London 1977

Perrero, L., *Alligators and Crocodiles of the World. The Disappearing Dragons*, Windward Publ. Inc., Miami 1975

Pritchard, P. C. H., *Encyclopaedia of Turtles*, T. F. H. Publ. Inc. Ltd, Jersey City 1979

Rimpp, K., *Salamander und Molche. Schwanzlurche im Terrarium*, Eugen Ulmer, Stuttgart 1985

Taylor, E. H., *The Caecilians of the World. A Taxonomic Review*, University of Kansas Press, Lawrence 1968

Works on amphibians and reptiles of various geographical areas
Amaral, A. (ed.), *Serpentes do Brasil. Iconografia colorida*. Edições Melhoramentos, Editora da Universidade de São Paulo, São Paulo 1977

Arnold, E. N., and Burton, J. A., *A Field Guide to the Reptiles and Amphibians of Britain and Europe*, William Collins & Sons, London 1978

Behler, J. L., and King, F. W., *The Audubon Society Field Guide to North American Reptiles and Amphibians*, Alfred A. Knopf, New York 1979

Berry, P. Y., *The Amphibian Fauna of Peninsular Malaysia*, Tropical Press, Kuala Lumpur 1975

Bohme, W. (ed.), (ongoing), *Handbuch der Reptilien und Amphibien Europas*, Vols 1, 2, 3, Akademische Verlagsgesellschaft, AULA Verlag, Wiesbaden 1981, 1984, 1986

Branch's, B., *Field Guide to the Snakes and Other Reptiles of Southern Africa*, New Holland Publishers Ltd, London 1988

Cogger, H. G., *Reptiles and Amphibians of Australia* (third edition), A. H. and A. W. Reed, Sidney 1983

Conant, R., *A Field Guide to Reptiles and Amphibians of Eastern and Central North America* (second edition), Houghton Mifflin Co., Boston 1975

Cook, F. R., *Introduction to Canadian Amphibians and Reptiles*, National Museums of Canada, Ottawa 1984

Daniel, J. C., *The Book of Indian Reptiles*, Bombay Natural History Society, Bombay 1983

De Haas, C. P. J., *Checklist of the Snakes of the Indo-Australian Archipelago (Reptiles, Ophidia)*, Linnaeus Press, Amsterdam 1972

Kampen, P. N. Van, *The Amphibia of the Indo-Australian Archipelago*, E. J. Brill, Leiden 1923

Lanza, B., *Guide per il riconoscimento delle specie animali delle acque interne italiane, 27, Anfibi, Rettili (Amphibia, Reptilia)*, C.N.R., Rome

Nakamura, K., and Ueno, S. I., *Japanese Reptiles and Amphibians in Colour*, Hoikuska Publishing Co., Osaka 1971

Passmore, N. I., and Carruthers, V. C., *South African Frogs*, Witwatersrand University Press, Johannesburg 1979

Pope, C. H., *The Reptiles of China*, American Museum of Natural History, New York 1935

Robb, *New Zealand Amphibians and Reptiles in Colour*, William Collins Publishers, Auckland 1980

Roze, J. A., *La Taxonomia y Zoogeografia de los Ofidios en Venezuela*, Universidad Central de Venezuela Ediciones de la Biblioteca, Caracas 1975

Schwartz, A. and Thomas, R., *A Check-list of West Indian Amphibians and Reptiles*, Carnegie Museum of Natural History Special Publication number 1, Pittsburgh 1975

Smith, H. M., and Smith R. B., (ongoing), *Synopsis of the Herpetofauna of Mexico*, vols 1–6, Erig Lundberg, Augusta 1971–1980

Stebbins, R. C., *A Field Guide to Western Reptiles and Amphibians* (second edition), Houghton Mifflin Co., Boston 1985

Stewart, M. M., *Amphibians of Malawi*, State University of New York Press, Albany, New York 1967

Thorn, R., *Les salamandres d'Europe, d'Asie et d'Afrique du Nord, Description et moeurs de toutes les espèces et sous-espèces d'Urodèles de la Région Palearctique d'après l'état de 1967*, P. Lechevalier, Paris 1969

Tweedie, M. W. F., *The Snakes of Malaya*, Singapore National Printers, Singapore 1983

Villiers, A., *Les serpents de l'ouest africain*, Les Nouvelles Editions Africaines, Université de Dakar, Initiations et Etudes Africaines n. 2, Dakar 1975

Welch, K. R. G., *Herpetology of Africa: a Checklist and Bibliography*, Krieger Publishing Co., Malabar 1982

Welch, K. R. G., *Herpetology of Europe and Southwest Asia: a Checklist and Bibliography*, Krieger Publishing Co., Malabar 1983

INDEX